The
MIND'S
ADVENTURE

The
MIND'S
ADVENTURE

Religion and Higher Education

HOWARD LOWRY

Philadelphia

THE WESTMINSTER PRESS

PREFACE

THE PLAN OF this book is a simple one. It begins
with an analysis of our contemporary situation, of
some of the ideas and influences that have brought
us where we are, midway in the century, and of the bearing of all this on colleges and universities. Then in the
second chapter there follows, not an account of the growth
of higher learning in America, or even of the colleges
founded by the Church, but the story of how and why religion that brought forth most higher education in this
country yielded its place very widely to the secular spirit.
The Harvard Report, *General Education in a Free Society,*
is examined as a part of this story, as are some recent educational trends and their significance.

The heart of the book is probably Chapter III, which
considers the relations of religion and education. Can a
liberal education include religion and remain what it is
supposed to be? If, on the other hand, it ignores religion,
can it, in the nature of things, be liberal at all? Anyone
who knows our contemporary campus scene knows the re-
awakened and vital interest in these questions, just as he
also knows that one small book will not exhaust any treatment of them. Chapter IV, on the Church college, is but

the second part of this same discussion. It is not a case study in any sense. It is rather an analysis of the nature of those colleges, whose influence in American life is out of all proportion to their size, that have the task of trying to be true to their religious purpose and at the same time be genuine places of higher learning and free inquiry.

The last chapter looks forward to the second half of our century and to the part education may or may not have in achieving some of our democratic goals. It tries to suggest also the kind of Christianity likely to have much significance for education and for human living.

The book deals only with colleges and universities, and leaves untouched the vexed question of the general role of State and Church in public education — a problem less troubling, incidentally, at the college and university level, where there is allegedly a greater level of maturity, than at the level of the elementary and secondary schools. Some matters treated here have, to be sure, great bearing on the general question. Any thoughtful college officer or teacher knows that what happens to young people of pre-college age crucially affects all higher learning. He knows how relatively unimportant he is compared with those who deal with boys and girls before he sees them.

It will be obvious that by the term ' religion ' the writer is usually thinking of Christianity, though much of what is said here has bearing on other religions, as well, in their relation to education. Moreover, I have been encouraged to include in this book some passages from articles or addresses I have previously printed, for the most part as college brochures. Such passages are not put in quotation marks.

This book was written at the request of certain men and women who felt a need either for it or, perhaps more exactly, for something like it. Its engendering spirit was Dr. E. Fay Campbell, Director of the Division of Higher Education of the Board of Christian Education of the Presbyterian Church in the U. S. A., who in turn received the support of the Board itself and its General Secretary, Dr. Paul Calvin Payne. Dr. Campbell secured the co-operation of and gave much preliminary detail for consideration to a committee that crossed denominational lines. This group, students of religion and education, met with the author on two occasions — once for a day and a half — for detailed discussion. I am indebted to them for all manner of help, and to some of them for detailed criticism of the manuscript. None of them is to be held responsible, of course, for any particular view here taken, as the author was allowed every freedom of thought and expression.

The members of the committee were: Ralph W. Lloyd, chairman; Frank H. Caldwell, Rex S. Clements, Arthur H. Compton, Arthur G. Coons, L. S. Cozart, John R. Cunningham, Miss Eleanor French, Harry M. Gage, Charles W. Gilkey, Theodore M. Greene, John O. Gross, Mrs. William A. Hastings, Paul S. Havens, Ralph C. Hutchison, Mrs. Joseph H. Kindle, Kenneth Latourette, H. Ganse Little, Hermann N. Morse, Norman B. Nash, George F. Thomas, and John A. Visser. Others joining their discussion included: Robert Cadigan, J. Leroy Dodds, William W. Hall, Jr., H. Gary Hudson, Walter Jenkins, Franc L. McCluer, Paul Meacham, Morgan S. Odell, Edward B. Paisley, Paul C. Payne, John Coventry Smith, and Paul R. Stewart. Miss Anne Horner, of the Board of Christian Education, acted as secretary of the committee.

I am indebted to the officers of The Westminster Press and especially to Mrs. Kathryn E. Wagner and her associates in the editorial department.

Any thoughts or feelings I have about education owe so much to colleagues I have had at Princeton University and at The College of Wooster that I could not begin to detail the obligation.

I am grateful also to the Board of Trustees of The College of Wooster for time given me from administrative duties, and to my colleague, Dean Henry William Taeusch, for carrying tasks beyond his portion. My particular thanks must go to Curt N. Taylor, Secretary of The College of Wooster, without whose help many people's work, my own especially, would not get done.

H. L.

The College of Wooster,
January 3, 1950.

CONTENTS

The
MIND'S
ADVENTURE

CHAPTER
1

HALFWAY IN THE CENTURY

ONE HUNDRED YEARS AGO all England was agog with preparation for the Great Exhibition at the Crystal Palace. It was to mark, when realized a few months later, the triumph of international production, industry, and art in the middle of the nineteenth century. With Mr. Darwin's troubling thoughts about our origin still eight years away, man was free to celebrate in pride and in hope the record of his no mean glory. Four thousand tons of iron, four hundred tons of glass, and six hundred thousand cubic feet of lumber went into a vast building where, on the opening day, Prince Albert, whose dream it all was, handed to Queen Victoria the enormous catalogue of the exhibition, to the prayers of the Archbishop of Canterbury and the singing of four choirs. In little over five months some six million people came to stare at the nineteen thousand evidences that man had been very busy in admirable and amazing ways. The Crystal Palace itself was not the least of his glories. And, we are told,[1] nothing more pleased the visitors than certain elm trees which, spared by the builders, now towered inside the glass frame up toward the high galleries.

A century later we could easily have our own exhibition.

It would dwarf the older one to pygmy size. Proliferating itself over land, sea, and air, the genius and industry of man has struck the older epochs silent with its impressive list of wonders. Only the dour and perverse could be ungrateful for all that might now be revealed in some Plastic Palace Exhibition of 1950. Any wholesale cavil, unmindful of what has been done for us by the marvels now common in our life, would be as ungenerous as the highly spiritual lecturer who is caught damning science to the thousands by means of the radio or as the clergyman in northern Scotland who complained that his new dictaphone was good enough save that it had the worst Aberdeen accent he had ever heard.

But men can be both grateful and wistful at the same time. They can also be sick and troubled in their souls. In the year 1950 there is more first-class concern — some of it panicky, some anxious but determined — than at any other time in our century. Thoughtful people have been saying some very plain things about our present state and our future direction; they feel a deep crisis in human affairs. And, if society in general has grown more concerned about itself, so has education. If any elm trees were left standing in the twentieth century's great exhibition hall, beneath them would be discovered some very troubled educators. For it is no longer news that in the last ten years more frank and widespread self-examination has gone on in American higher education than we have ever seen before. Educators have dealt with leading ideas instead of gadgets. They have special care about what we are all doing, what we think we are, where we intend to go, and the faith by which we live. They have seen that what is good and bad in society has been — or will be — good and bad in education. They know also that all this works the

other way round. They suspect that colleges and universities, like the rest of the world, have concentrated on
means, to a disregard of ends. 'Where shall wisdom be
found? And where is the place of understanding?' Where
are all of us halfway in the century?

Dean Inge told us very plainly. To him this is 'the century of disappointment.' Many less downright than he
would say substantially the same. There is a sense of high
chances missed in international relations, of some need of
unifying forces deeper than 'a common impulse for the
same money,' of something very dry or very muddled in
the spirit of man. Optimistic writers who once had a formula for setting everything right have grown disillusioned.
The late H. G. Wells, we are reminded,[2] only a few years
ago was pinning his faith to science as 'an avalanche
which will cleanse the world.' But shortly before his death
he renounced this 'odd metaphor' in favor of thorough
despair. Even those who are not philosophers, even those
not troubled daily by thoughts of war or of some impend-
ing cosmic halloween full of dark witchery and fear,
have nevertheless a sense of something askew in our situation. They are exemplified best, perhaps, in the British
workman whom Dorothy Sayers [3] tells of. Reflecting on
the contemporary scene, he concluded, 'We're being had
for mugs,' a Saxon way of implying that somehow we have
been badly taken in. Others, more deeply critical, have a
deeper indictment. They see our century, fresh from two
world tragedies, trying to write the script for another.
They see the perilous balance of the quite literal choice
we have between life and death; the choice, as Mr. Eliot
puts it, of 'fire or fire' — the fire of our own devilish in-
genuity or the fire of reason and divine love which con-
sumes the other fire and transfigures whatever it touches

for noble and human ends. One of the most thoughtful
modern historians has suggested that civilization now finds
itself where John Bunyan's Christian found himself almost three centuries ago: ' I dreamed, and behold I saw
a man cloathed with rags, standing in a certain place, with
his face from his own house, a book in his hand, and a
great burden upon his back. I looked, and saw him open
the book and read therein; and as he read he wept and
trembled; and, not being able longer to contain, he broke
out with a lamentable cry saying " What shall I do? " ' [4]

No one likely to look at this book needs instruction in
the issues of our time. We all know how the years that
have followed World War II have carried off a good many
corners of our hope, though to the strong and persevering
they suggest merely the magnitude of what we yet have
to do. We know, moreover, the way things have been
squarely put to education. We know it is now too dangerous to let the learned run amuck if all they have is
technical information. We recognize the essential truth
of Justice Robert Jackson's striking summary: ' It is one
of the paradoxes of our time that modern society needs to
fear . . . only the educated man. The primitive peoples
of the earth constitute no menace. The most serious crimes
against civilization can be committed only by educated
and technically competent people.' We are trying to give
Dr. Jekyll a companion now and confer the doctor's degree
also on Mr. Hyde, on those who would freely use or be indifferent to the use of learning for brutish ends. To em-
bellish all this would be to light a candle to demonstrate
the sun.

Even so, if we are to follow the considerations about
higher education raised in the following pages we can help
ourselves by reviewing and by trying to catch the total

effect of the leading currents and contending influences of our time. What things have brought us, mid-century, to where we are?

However sensible our judgment, however tired we may be of the facile prophets of our doom, some basic figures will not be silenced. In the fifty years just ending we have staged a mass slaughter outgoing all the previous history. We have had in all these years scarcely one year without war. As Professor Quincy Wright has shown, European powers alone fought seventy-four wars during the first thirty years of our century, wars lasting a total of 297 years, the average four years long. From the eleventh to the twentieth century war casualties totaled roughly eighteen million. In the first three decades only of our century we killed thirty-three and a third per cent more human beings than were killed in the previous eight hundred years — and these figures do not include five continents or World War II and its prelude. Citing these grim tables, the dean of the Harvard Graduate School observes:

If any human being brought up in the tradition of western civilization could, by some miracle, step outside the familiar patterns of that culture; if history could come to him with the same shock of surprise that a new and stimulating novel brings him; if, in sum, retaining the moral idealism of western civilization as a standard of measurement, he could yet discover for the first time what has happened to mankind in the last fifty years, such a person would, I think, be overwhelmed by a single tragic conviction; namely, that the history of mankind for the last half century has been a history of deepening horror. . . .

If the entire population of the United States were

wiped out tomorrow, their number would be less than the number of human beings who have died of violence, disease, or starvation in war or as a result of it during the last half century. It doesn't make sense.[5]

The turn has been called on us. Science, which has been 'putting the miraculous into circulation' and suggesting that nothing is so strange and daring that mankind may not achieve it, has put another surprise squarely in our faces:

We have acquired a unique power, the inverse of all others. We have become able to blow up this planet, together with mankind and mankind's power of creating power. It is a solemn moment. Until now it could not be said that mankind was the master of its future, for it was still *condemned* to a future, although each individual could put a bullet through his head any time he liked. Now mankind will have to choose; and it will have to make an heroic effort not to choose the easy way out — suicide. One might say that it begins its maturity from this moment.[6]

As Dr. Arthur H. Compton has insisted since the summer of 1945, 'Atomic power is forcing mankind into a greater humanity.'

Confronting the period of our enforced 'maturity,' what do we recognize as having been the marks of our adolescence? First of all, a temptation to concentrate on means and ignore ends, to believe that whatever worked was right. We had a childish willingness to go on making things without any standards of value. We failed to see that behind all human work are human beings who themselves bring all good and bad to light; that

Whatever flames upon the night
Man's own resinous heart has fed.[7]

This moral relativism has had in it plenty of mischief for
both society and for individuals. It was interesting not
long ago to watch the fervent response of both old and
young to the late Peter Marshall's prayer in the Senate,
where it doubtless did good: ' Give us the courage to stand
for something lest we fall for everything.' For, as a people,
we have widely held the fancy though naïve belief that
we could go on contriving, piling up, feeling, enjoying,
and gorging — losing ourselves in phenomena without
long-range standards of discrimination. If anything went
wrong, it was not the failure of a leading idea; it was
thought merely to be the lack of one more material ele-
ment — not the missing mind and soul, but the missing
gadget. One of our more discerning newspaper editors
recently wrote in his wry fashion: ' After a lunch of spikes,
coins, tacks, a bullet, golf ball, knife handle, bottle stop-
per, spoon, and can opener a zoo ostrich dies in Britain.
The lack of proteins will get anyone in time.'[8] Indiscrim-
inate diet affects men as well as ostriches. Our ' combination of physical power and moral and social waywardness '
is now ' the crisis of the twentieth century. It was manifest
after the first World War. It is even more manifest after
the last one. We have reached the stage where we know
how to do almost anything, but have lost track of *why*
anything we do should be done.'[9]

This neutrality between right and wrong has naturally
been part of the academic world too. Yet no indictment of
relativism has been sharper than that given by an academic man, one of the keenest of our critics: ' The denial
of value judgments — the doctrine that good is merely a

convenient mask for self-aggrandisement and evil whatever checks or lessens the superiority of myself, my race,
clique or party — this surely is a poison superior to anything chemical warfare has yet contrived.' [10] Modern relativism came to full and bitter fruit on August 22, 1939,
almost the day of its apotheosis, when Adolf Hitler assem-
bled his top brass and iron in his eagle-circled retreat at
Berchtesgaden and told his generals what was on his mind
as Von Ribbentrop was flying to Russia for the fateful pact
with Stalin: ' I shall give a propagandistic justification for
starting the war. Never mind whether it makes sense or
not. No one will ask the victor whether or not he told the
truth. In starting the war it is not right that matters but
victory. . . . The way is open for the soldier. Our strength
is in our quickness and in our brutality.' [11] Thus went the
new German version of what makes ' a mighty fortress.'
It was merely the ugly outgrowth of what for years had
been the dominant creed of the twentieth century.

Moral relativism has been, of course, the product of our
secularism. Gaining steadily in men's minds for four centuries, though its roots are as old as history, secularism
holds that this life on earth as man knows it is the bound
of all he can or needs to know. Without reference to any
divine power, he can work out his deliverance by wisely
using the resources he has at hand. Anything transcending
human life is no longer needed. It is, in fact, an illusion
to be ignored or despised. A ' satisfactory human existence
is not an affair of nature, man, and God; it is altogether
an affair of nature, man, and society. Thus contemporary
secularism is both a protest against the need of anything
akin to the Christian faith, and a policy and program of
living which claim that " human society is ultimate and
human ills are curable by it." It is within this secular frame

of reference that contemporary man chiefly lives, moves, and charts his history.' [12]

Secularism gives room, of course, to varieties of creeds within itself. It has accommodated many philosophies of the last hundred years: positivism, limiting knowledge to scientifically verifiable experience; empiricism, whose ultimate standard is the report of the senses; pragmatism, whose test is whatever works; Nietzscheism, with its exaltation of power and its ultimate god of the superman; agnosticism, of the kind professed by Herbert Spencer, who tripped himself up logically by holding that his only knowledge was that he had no knowledge. It included behaviorism, its heyday now many years past, explaining all our highest aspirations and workings in convenient mechanistic terms, till its whole validity was finally scuttled by the common-sense realization on a great many people's part that a *thinking* behaviorist simply couldn't be — that he was a contradiction of his own theory. Secularism entertained gladly the general mechanistic view of science which the best scientists have now shot full of holes. All along, the common man had a hunch that the thoroughgoing mechanist was in a bad way, since, his thought being the phase of a machine and therefore not thought at all, the mechanist always faced the melancholy embarrassment of knowing that he could not possibly have decided what he had just decided.

Secularism includes, moreover, two general views of human nature that have had their followers over the years. One of these is naturalism, which rests its faith in a scientific account of life but has its emotional roots in the belief that man is but the spoiled child of nature. The beginnings of this belief are very old, but its most flaming expression came after Rousseau's vision on the road from

Paris to Vincennes in 1749, when there flashed on his feverish, susceptible mind the belief that man is naturally good and became wicked only through our institutions — a charming idyll, somewhat odd in its logic if one remembers that institutions are made by man and therefore reflect his nature. A great deal of trouble followed this sentimental view of man's natural *bonté* or goodness. One critic of Rousseau used to call it merely 'romanticism on all fours.' The contemporary believer in naturalism has largely dropped the lyrical note of Rousseau. He is, indeed, likely to be an informed, sincere person who likes to get good things done in the world and feels we get nowhere by trucking with starry-eyed supernaturalism and religion.

Secularism includes also the quite different view, that of humanism, which sees man as the creature of reason, with standards and checks within his breast upon his naturalistic, animal tendencies. Its whole faith is in the ordering of life by reason and the higher nature that marks men off from beasts. As Panofsky has pointed out, humanism is a kind of mean between the two extremes of *barbaritas* and *divinitas* and keeps up a two-front war with both. It places man above nature by virtue of powers granted him alone; but, like naturalism, it holds no need of such a God as Christianity proclaims. To the humanist, Jesus need be only a remarkably good man influencing other men to be good. He and they require no other sanction.

Christianity has, of course, often been unfair in its refusal to acknowledge the good things secularism has done. Reacting against the ancient and modern sins of the Church — ignorance, bigotry, sentimentality, blindness to practical needs — secularism has accomplished its own fine work. It has fought for civil liberties, universal education, the free play of ideas, and scientific method. It has healed diseases, cleaned up whole areas of social wrong, and given its own set of wings to men's minds and their creative working. In industry, the arts, and all the higher regions of our life save one, its gains have been great. It has even aided religion by forcing religion to many a re-examination of itself. It saw the ways in which religion, misapplied or corrupted, had stifled human progress and felt as Voltaire did at Ferney when, a church blocking his view, he pulled it down that he might see properly. Secularism in its higher forms was fed up with professedly religious people who, like the mother in Sidney Howard's play *The Silver Cord,* methodically messed up everything around her while she kept the 'Little Flowers' of Saint Francis — which deserved a better fate — on her night table. It was sick of pious aggrandizements, of selfishness going out in the name of religion — going out, as it was grimly said of certain misguided imperialists, to do good and ending up by doing well.

It is equally fair to notice, however — and academic men, in particular, have never noticed it enough — that much of the best in secularism is a Christian by-product. After two thousand years it is very hard, indeed, even to say what is secular and what is not. The emancipated free-thinker, scornful of religion, lives off an ethical code that still borrows from the faith of his fathers. The Christian heritage shines everywhere on men who scarcely realize what is shining on them. In all walks of life, in science and industry, in the learned professions, and in the homeliest of their duties, people make sacrifices and give consecrated service to others out of instincts derived often from a for-gotten religious idealism of which they themselves would say they were ashamed. Men who no longer go to church would not willingly live in a community where there were no churches. Everywhere society passes a noble coinage that denies the mint from which it came, and a great part of our spiritual capital is borrowed from a bank men no longer believe to exist. Our democratic faith, for example, will always bear the stamp of a religion that has fed it through the years. Men who work sincerely for human brotherhood are not apparently bothered by their illogical — and highly unnatural — conception of brothers without a common father. Few things annoy the secularist more, of course, than the Christian's reminder that the Father-hood of God is the logical condition of any real brother-hood of man. Nor should the Christian, for that matter, shut his own eyes stubbornly to the secular possibilities of the social gains arising solely from increased awareness of a common lot of men that must somehow be better, what-ever the relationships of men may basically be. Even so, it would be cleaner linguistically if the secularist would think up some other term to describe the essential mu-tuality of all of us and stop using a nostalgic term like 'brotherhood,' a term loaded with logic and love. His failure to do so reflects the noble confusion that surrounds us in these important matters.

We can hardly even estimate properly that ancient Greek world where secular humanism finds so much of its origin. We are told this Greek world would have been enough for our guidance — that it would have given us a clearer Western culture than the Hebraic world gave us; that, in Ezra Pound's rather nasty phrase, the very idea of Jehovah was 'a Semitic cuckoo's egg laid in the Eu-ropean nest.' This Greek world, especially as Aristotle worked things out in Plato's light, would have given us all the ethics, all the higher values, we can properly use. To

that Greek civilization, which still gives light and leading
to our education, we all, of course, stand debtor. But even
here we cannot, in the year 1950, exactly judge effects.
Nor can the most ardent Hellenist, try as he will, keep
Athens free of Jerusalem. A Christian coloring falls on the
classic pages. We read Plato on love as the working principle of life, and the very text as we read takes added luster
from the great thirteenth chapter of First Corinthians,
which most of us knew in childhood, long before we heard
of Plato. The *Republic*'s view of order as the basis for
society — of a music in the affairs of men that we either
augment or spoil — finds readers prepared for it by having
long heard of 'members all of one body,' baptized into it
by 'one Spirit . . . , whether we be Jews or Gentiles,
whether we be bond or free.' And that most memorable
of Plato's writings, his account of the trial and death of
Socrates, borrows a singular heightening from another
trial and death of which most of us heard before we were
five years old. Even on the ancient world that preceded
it Christianity now casts backward its own distinctive
light.

But humanism, assisted or not, keeps a debit as well
as a credit column in its ledger, as has been said of ' scientific progress ' generally. And the debit side, the failure of
all secularism as a guide to man's life, is the red and tragic
failure of the first half of our century. The most superficial
observer can see what it has helped to bring about: a dilut-
ing of important ethical standards, vulgarization of whole
areas of life, preposterous lusts for power, and the greatest
mass destruction in history. It has, for lack of ultimate
standards, allowed ' the strange pseudo-absolutes of the
god-state, the superior race,' the totalitarian society of
materialism.[18] It has helped to produce the society Lewis

Mumford has described as ours: ' the modern world with
its over-charges of empty stimuli, its perpetual miscarriage
of technique, its materialistic repletion, its costly ritual of
conspicuous waste, its highly organized purposelessness.' [14]

The tragic lack of values and sanctions in secularism
arises from the almost paradoxical principles it holds. Its
relativism comes from its renouncement of eternal, divine
values; but it comes also from the secularist's free-wheel-
ing optimism about the nature of man. Scornful of wishful thinking, he seems at times the most giddy of wishful
thinkers. For, if he turns from the City of God, he has an
almost winsome trust in the City of Man. His optimism
stems from the French philosophers of the eighteenth century and their idea of indefinite human progress. Consist-
ency was not their jewel. ' They renounced the authority
of church and Bible, but exhibited a naïve faith in the
authority of nature and reason. They scorned metaphysics,
but were proud to be called philosophers. They disman-
tled heaven, somewhat prematurely it seems, since they
retained their faith in the immortality of the soul. They
courageously discussed atheism, but not before the serv-
ants. . . . They denied that miracles ever happened, but
believed in the perfectibility of the human race.' [15]

Secularism has about itself a seeming modesty — a willingness to move patiently from fact to fact, a dread of
high-flown assumptions. It numbers in its ranks many un-
selfish and genuinely humble men. But as a creed it is
committed to a pride in man's self-sufficiency that the
Greeks knew was the tragic flaw in life and that Christianity has described as ' sin.' To a Christian the down-to-
earth, here-and-now realism of the secularist isn't realism
at all. To him there is a more acute account of human nature in the Christian view of man as a creature of two

sides, in whom the elements are strangely mixed — marred
yet not wholly corrupt, since he is at least uncorrupt
enough to suspect his own corruption. In his wayward
dualism, he is 'the glory, jest, and riddle of the world.'
Longing for personal identity, a haunting homelessness
within his blighted but aspiring soul, he senses a standard
beyond himself. He thinks the answer to his riddles does
not lie within his own double-talk nature or the surrounding double-talk earth. In the mirror of his present knowledge he sees the quivering image of himself, incomplete,
unsatisfied. In his heart is some hint of everlasting laws.
In the religion he professes, he finds validation for belief,
renewal for himself, a place for his lasting loyalties in
Christ, who reveals to him what God is. For he holds it
not irreverent to think of a reverse side to the very incarnation. In that great moment in history when we saw for the
first time a man without sin, when we saw death become
life before men's eyes, when the very God appeared, not
in the form of some fanatic but in a person of reasonableness and charm — a man who could move among men and
feel utterly at home with them and they with him, one
who bore about himself 'no strangeness whatever except
the strangeness of perfection' — it was not just the incarnation of his God. In a deep and awful sense it was his
own also. The Word was made flesh, but the flesh was
also made Word, sharing the mark of the Spirit behind all
living. The Christian sees here the revelation of a love in
which his own defects are lost; but he sees also the suggestion of a hard-working, practical partnership with eternal goodness, a call to meaningful effort in the world at
hand. The pattern of this effort is no relative thing, something in his ephemeral custody alone, nor even in the custody of the race. It is a pattern with everlasting sanction

behind it, the justice and law and love of God its deep-struck seal and shining point of reference. If all these things a Christian holds as truth are a strain upon the patience and imagination of the secularist, it is no more amazing burden on credulity than his own secular belief, entirely unsupported by experience, that by his unaided hand man can achieve something that, were he to achieve it, would turn him into the very god he refuses to recognize. To the Christian, man's claim to any such divinity seems a fiction more absurd than any religion, in its wildest moments of distortion, has suggested. He sees the secularist showing himself once again all the kingdoms of the world in a moment of time. He remembers when this very thing was done once before.

Thus it is — and it is becoming clearer — that modern society and educated men, especially, have to choose between the secular and the sacred view of life. In this choice they have awareness of the chief weakness of secularism. Its relative values at their best have no adequate sanction for enforcing them among men. Secularism needs the constant support and heightening of ideas higher than any of its own. Even the agnostic knows the power of religious conceptions in lifting men out of barbarism and ' must admit that if he himself cannot accept these truths, he must at least recognize them as indispensable pragmatic figments without which civilization cannot exist.' [16] He knows, moreover, that when these truths ' worked ' they worked not as ' pragmatic figments ' but as something believed true. Men acted upon them because they cherished them in their hearts as real. All the sanction is in this. As old President Patton used to say at Princeton, ' You can't make a boy moral merely by spraying him two hours a week with a course in ethics.' The ' religious attitudes' and 'ideal social goals' that John Dewey and other noble secularists long for arise from standards more deeply rooted than any secularism has to offer. The humanists 'are, in Dr. Niebuhr's phrase, "children of light." But against the "children of darkness" they have no effective defence.' [17]

The late William Temple, one of the most social-minded of churchmen, naturally sympathized with all the best in humanism. But he saw its essential weakness when it tried to bind men to high values and high action. Speaking of the allegedly Christian civilization in England up to the Second World War, he said:

> For at least half a century its predominate culture has been what is called Humanism, which consists, roughly speaking, in the acceptance of many Christian standards of life with a rejection or neglect of the only sources of power to attain to them. The result was a decline from those standards in all respects in which conformity to them involved serious self-discipline.[18]

Secular societies pay tribute to this moving power of Christian sanctions by keeping Christian forms and phrases. Some have wondered whether, if we were now starting our currency, the America of 1950 would stamp 'In God We Trust' upon its coins. Were that sentence abandoned, it is interesting to speculate on what the substitute might be. Strictly speaking, the true secular legend should be 'In Ourselves We Trust.' But secularism has too much humor — and perhaps the check of some deeper instinct — to put it there. Men have trouble finding, either seriously or humorously, within their unaided, undirected selves alone, the transforming something that produces a good life on earth.

If secularism, with its lack of ultimate values, has hurt society, it has hurt individuals also. It has left many scientists to be the victims of their 'scientism' and discouraged them from true philosophy and a total view of life. It has let them think that science is all there is. It has encouraged in them the charming fiction that 'human culture, institutions, every living thing and all that proceeds from life, all change of whatever character, can be weighed, measured, calculated, and the direction and amount of change or growth predicted.' [19] It has allowed specialists to be specialists without first trying to be men. Worse yet, it has permitted them to generalize from insufficient perspective, to everyone's confusion. And, quite apart from these things, it has produced that twentieth-century creation par excellence, 'the hollow man.'

This 'hollow man,' the spiritual product of our secular wasteland, is the dry spectator, for whom life seems to be little more than what Clarence Darrow once said it was, 'an unpleasant interruption of nothingness.' He chooses no sides, knows nothing of the joy of contending for good causes. Without anchor for himself or direction either, he remains the neutral observer. He has a passion for security — often on a fairly low level — rather than for pioneering. Absent from all values, he is absent from himself as well. And his less thoughtful counterpart is the average sensual materialist, whose life is a matter of addition and things. Whenever his material world blows up, he is like the unfortunate greyhounds before whose eyes the mechanical rabbit they were chasing exploded on a Florida dog track not long ago. The end of life vanished in thin air before them, their bewilderment was complete. They share in a vast contemporary scene, a land where 'things are in the saddle' and ride no small portion of mankind, a land over

which, in the poet's bitter prophecy, the wind may someday blow and say,

> 'Here were decent godless people:
> Their only monument the asphalt road
> And a thousand lost golf balls.' [20]

Life and education are, or should be, the pursuit of significance, which, as *Life*'s 'Round Table' discovered some
months ago, in a sudden inspiration, is what we really
mean by 'the pursuit of Happiness.' What makes us live
is whatever enhances our capacity to confer a meaning on
what we know and feel in our given span of years. All
learning that is not pedantry becomes this quest of significance. It gives the power to seek this significance with
clarity, patience, range, commitment, and distinction. But
this quest requires a scale of high values and the highest
faith possible to man. Secularism has not furnished an
adequate sense of these values or an adequate drive toward them.

Small wonder that educators, looking at what men
choose for themselves and the values they honor in the
middle of the century, are asking as never before: 'What
do we honor and nourish in our schools and colleges?'
'What chance do the highest values have there for adequate study or expression?' They know how vital colleges
and universities are in giving leading ideas to our national
life — all down the line. They know that education is even-
tually a kind of dynamite. They have clearly seen that
'education is the most Fascist aspect of the Fascist Revolution, the most Communist feature of the Communist
Revolution, and the most Nazi expression of the National
Socialist Revolution.' [21] They now realize with new force
that 'the moral, intellectual, and spiritual reformation for

which the world waits depends, then, upon true and deeply held convictions about the nature of man, the ends of life, the purposes of the state, and the order of goods.' [22] They wonder if higher education has given decent room to the beliefs that have fostered the great convictions of the Western world.

Not all educators, by any means, are rushing toward a revival of religion. Secularism has rarely had more triumphant and less scientifically chastened expression than that given by Julian Huxley,* conspicuously in the forefront of UNESCO and therefore presumably no mean spokesman for what some men want education to be throughout the world: 'The advance of natural science, logic, and psychology has brought us to a stage at which God is no longer a useful hypothesis . . . a faint trace of God still broods over the world like the smile of a cosmic Cheshire cat. But the growth of psychological knowledge will rub even that from the universe.' [23] A host of other educators, however, see the matter in another light. An-

---

* This might seem the natural sentiment of Thomas Huxley's grandson. But Thomas Huxley, for all his agnosticism and devotion to science in the face of an often hostile Church, once said in a debate on introducing the Bible into the schools of London: ' I always was in favor of a secular education in our public schools — I mean an education without theology. But I am greatly embarrassed when I must answer the question, " By what practical means the religious spirit — which is the main foundation of all mortality in the present chaotic confusion of opinions — can be sustained without the assistance of the Bible? " Nowhere is the fundamental truth that the welfare of the state in the long run depends upon the welfare of the citizen as strongly laid down. The human race is not yet, possibly never may be, in a position to dispense with it. . . . If for my own children I had to choose between a school in which true religion is taught and one without religion I would prefer the former.' — *Quoted by Henry H. Sweets, Source Book on Christian Education, p. 35. Presbyterian Church in the U.S., 1942.*

other distinguished scientist, who is also a Christian, the dean of the Graduate School at Princeton, finds notable the rallying of Western scholars of every type to a new defense of spiritual values. He cites, among others, Sir Edmund Whittaker, the mathematician, who concludes that ' the deeper understanding of the material universe, which has been achieved by scientific discovery, has opened up new prospects and possibilities to the advocate of belief in God.' [24]

The charge now deepens in many quarters that education has not led in nourishing the highest values society needs; that it has even refused a full consideration of what the values suggested by Christianity are and of what Christianity itself is. 'The universities have given the world the guidance it needed in science, economics, and sociology, but not in the knowledge of good and evil. Hence they have failed to help civilization where it most needs help.' [25] Norman Cousins thinks the term 'higher education' has, in fact, become a misnomer, not so much through the fault of the educator as through history, which 'stopped crawling about eighty years ago and began to catapult.' The danger he sees is the one Whitehead saw — that man would be outrun by events and left 'a panting and helpless anachronism.' 'We have leaped centuries ahead in inventing a new world to live in, but as yet we have an inadequate conception of our part in that world. We have surrounded and confounded ourselves with gaps — gaps between revolutionary science and evolutionary anthropology, between cosmic gadgets and human wisdom, between intellect and conscience. The clash between knowledge and ethics that Henry Thomas Buckle foresaw a century ago is now more than a mere skirmish.' [26]

Woodrow Wilson was never fooled on this score — aus-

tere lover of learning though he was. He honored the mind
as few men ever have, but he steadily saw that the mind
was directly involved with forces even more potent in
their immediate effect. ' We speak of this age,' he said, ' as
an age when mind is monarch, but I take it for granted
that if that is true, mind is one of those monarchs who
reigns but does not govern. As a matter of fact, the world
is governed in every generation by a great House of Commons made up of the passions; and we can only be careful
to see that the handsome passions are in the majority.' [27]
He would have endorsed the view that, if American education has failed in leadership, it has failed because of its
own confusion about what should lead us and because of
its excluding too often from the circle of its own ideas one
of the greatest, if not the greatest, considerations on man
and his destiny.

The task of education is always a double one. It must
make two simultaneous efforts. True research will consist
in what secular learning honors without question, in the
scientific quest for new fact, without fear or favor; in the
attempt, as Goethe put it, ' to keep pressing our outposts
into the darkness and to establish no post that is not per-
fectly in light and firm.' But it will consist also in a second
task — one that education has in many places forgotten —
in a clear return and penetration into the abiding realities
made known to us in the humane past, in philosophy, in
history and religion, and in any consideration of the full
nature and heritage of man. It is the enlightenment of
human beings completely viewing their human situation.
Both these efforts are needed, the one to save and assist
the other. When either part of this joint enterprise breaks
down, one has something less universal than a university,
something too small and too dangerous for the spirit of

man. This is no longer an academic matter. It is of crucial
concern for our common life. Too long higher education
has cut itself off from its great resources. H. S. Canby
wrote, in a memorable editorial in the spring of 1948:

> Even fifty years ago, as most of us know, the pipe
> lines from the great classics of our civilization had be-
> come clogged or broken. . . . The crisis arrived when
> after two wars it became tragically evident that in edu-
> cation we had burned bridges behind us. . . . It is
> essential — so essential that words cannot convey the
> penalty for failure — that the pipe lines to our stores of
> culture and religion shall be re-opened. . . . If one
> tenth of the imagination, the creative energy, and the
> sheer concentration of the intellect which has produced
> the atomic bomb had been devoted to retapping the an-
> cient waters of life, and finding *how* and *where* they
> could be made to flow in a world irrevocably changed
> by science, we might even now be able to exchange this
> despair [of many contemporary intellectuals] for hope.[28]

Charles Kettering, of General Motors, certainly one of
the most interesting men alive, has recently told us of the
effort his company once made to find an automobile spring
that would not break. Seven of the best spring makers in
the country assured him that no spring could stand more
than two thousand flexings. General Motors began their
own experiment, on a bar of steel eighteen inches long,
two inches wide, and a quarter of an inch thick. They gave
this metal a surface treatment of heavy blasts of shot, a
hail of small steel balls each about one sixteenth of an
inch in diameter. As Mr. Kettering put it, ' Somehow that
punishment makes the molecules in the steel clutch each
other with a new fervor, resulting in a tremendously

greater over-all toughness.' The steel bar so treated has withstood five hundred thousand flexings and shows no sign of breaking.

Here is both a symbol of our ingenious age and a symbol of what we yet have to become. Society too has been receiving its steady rain of shot over far too many years. It needs a new association. The human molecules must now turn to one another, to some common working, 'with a new kind of fervor.' Unlike molecules of steel, however, human molecules have passion, self-will, conceit, laziness, and — both worst and best of all — memory. But they have also admiration, hope, and love, and a turn toward excellence placed deep within them. They can be led out of prejudice and indifference, into the waking reality of their own best selves. They can transcend the materialism satirized by an American humorist quoting what we trust is a fictitious advertisement: ' Am thirty-eight years old. Would like to marry young woman of thirty who has a tractor. Please send picture of the tractor.' They can be made to love the right things for the right reasons. What education must propose to the last half of our century is a new revolt in the soul of man.

The prize this time is real. On every campus, as throughout the world, the trees of life and death stand side by side and for our choosing. Some ten years ago *Fortune* magazine gave, in substance, an unexpected and striking challenge to the Churches of America. Dr. Ganse Little, reporting for a commission of the Presbyterian Church in the U. S. A., passed it on to the 160th General Assembly: ' Unless the Church makes us hear a voice not our own voice, we shall all perish.'

The challenge is equally valid for colleges and universities — not just as a crudely important matter of survival, but as a matter of giving to human beings, in any time or season, the full life and stature that belongs to them. The voices we have largely been listening to have not been adequate voices, as more men come to see each day. Can we listen now to other voices, some that have been silenced or reduced to a whisper in many quarters of academic life? Can education give to religion the place it deserves? Can colleges and universities be open-minded enough to open their minds to the deepest questions raised by men and to thorough consideration of the classic answers given to these questions over the years? What have they done about this in the past? What are they doing now? Can they give religion a full expression in academic life and still keep the liberal character of true education and its intellectual integrity? How large can learning be?

These are living questions halfway in the century. They are all part, of course, of the question asked long ago and now become crucial in our time: ' Where shall wisdom be found? And where is the place of understanding? '

CHAPTER
2
___

VISION AND REVISION

After God had carried us safe to *New England,* and wee had builded our houses, provided necessaries for our liveli-hood, rear'd convenient places for Gods worship, and setled the Civill Government: One of the next things we longed for, and looked after was to advance *Learning* and perpetuate it to Posterity: dreading to leave an illiterate Ministery to the Churches, when our present Ministers shall lie in the Dust. And as wee were thinking and consulting how to effect this great Work; it pleased God to stir up the heart of one Mr. *Harvard* (a godly Gentleman, and a lover of Learning, there living amongst us).[1]

Here is the famous record, in its old form, of the first stake driven for higher education in America, driven but a few years after the landing of the *Mayflower.* It was driven by religion. To see the beginnings of Harvard in 1636 is to see at work the love of God and the desire to serve Him that brought nearly all the early colleges into being.

The one hundred or so religious men who thought and consulted about Harvard were graduates of the two great

English universities, chiefly Cambridge. The first Board of Overseers numbered six magistrates and six clergymen. And the very site of the new college was chosen partly because at what was then called Newtown lived the hardworking, devoted minister Thomas Shepard, 'the most powerful evangelical preacher in New England,' well liked by young men and described by a contemporary as one ' of whom it may be said, without any wrong to others, the Lord by his Ministery hath saved many a hundred soul.' [2]

Harvard's gifted historian has been careful to point out that we must not think of the early college as a ' theological seminary.' Actually it was less ecclesiastical than the English universities. In the Charter of 1650 its purpose is defined:

> The aduancement of all good literature, artes and Sciences.
> The aduancement and education of youth in all manner of good literature Artes and Sciences.
> All other necessary provisions that may conduce to the education of the English and Indian youth of this Country in knowledge: and godliness.

The term ' Artes and Sciences' meant merely ' the usual subjects of university study, and had no reference to what we call science.' [3] But Harvard thus sought early the balance of a liberal education. To be sure, the college was

> founded in *Christi Gloriam* and later dedicated *Christo et Ecclesiae.* Her presidents and tutors insisted that there could be no true knowledge or wisdom without Christ. Her founders dreaded ' to leave an illiterate Ministry to the Churches '; and but for the passionately sincere re-

ligion of these puritans, there would have been no
Harvard. But the intellectual fare that she provided for
young men was the old Liberal Arts course, with certain
changes made in the renaissance and reformation. Students destined for the ministry had to wait until after
taking the bachelor's degree before receiving any specialized training in theology.[4]

Yet Professor Morison agrees that 'the course was more
deeply impregnated with religion than that of any liberal
college today, because the puritan way of life brought
religion into every sphere.' The founders believed that
'all knowledge without Christ was vain.'[5] The learning
about God and Christ, 'which is eternal life,' was represented to students as 'the maine end of his life and studies' and 'the only foundation' of all sound learning. Private prayer was enjoined upon all students, and so was the
reading of the Scriptures twice a day. Even study and
attendance at lectures was thought of as 'redeeming the
time.' President Dunster warned his students often against
intellectual pride, which he felt had been the temptation
of his own youth: 'Take heed of this, least Desiring to be
as gods, we become as Deuills.'[6] Harvard represented, in
short, 'what the mother of Increase Mather said to her
son when he was an infant, that she desired God to give
him grace and learning. "Child," she said, "if God make
thee a Good Christian and a Good Scholar, thou hast all
that ever thy Mother Asked for thee."'[7]

There was no nonsense, either, in the application of
Harvard's lofty ideal. The first commencement of Septem-
ber 23, 1642, contained an oration in Greek, 'a Hebrew
Analysis Grammatical, Logicall and Rhetoricall' of The
Psalms, based on a Latin commentary. And at the meeting

of the Board of Overseers held that same afternoon complaint was made against ' two young men, of good quality, lately come out of England, for foul misbehavior, in swearing and ribaldry speeches, etc.' The Board gave the president authority to flog the offending students, and as soon as the festivities were over this was done.[8] The higher learning in America was in full stride.

This chapter is not an account of the development of Christian higher education in America. Nor, be it particularly noted, is it the story of the rise and growth of the Church colleges that have kept their central Christian purpose to this day. It is rather the story of how religion brought forth our colleges and universities and then yielded to the secular spirit. A glance at the early years in some of our best-known institutions will suggest the striking change.

In William Bradford's phrase, the small candle lit at Harvard lit a thousand. The religious impulse, sprung from Harvard or otherwise, was the influence behind the colonial colleges. William and Mary, founded in 1693, was Episcopalian in origin. Its moving spirit was Dr. James Blair, a Scot, and its first chancellor was the bishop of London. Then, at the turn of the century, ten Congregational ministers constituted themselves a board of trustees at New Haven. All but one of these fathers of Yale were Harvard men.

The founding of Yale was a direct answer to the secular spirit that began to make itself felt toward the end of the seventeenth century in a wide decline of faith and morals.[9] Abraham Pierson felt that in such a time he could not turn away from becoming the first rector of the new college. Although four fifths of all Pierson's students became ministers, Yale shared Harvard's desire also to form devoted

Christian laymen. It gave instruction in the 'arts and sciences' that youth, through the blessing of Almighty God 'may be fitted for Public employment both in Church & Civil State.'

The moving chapter in Yale's earlier religious history is not so much that of the Great Awakening of 1740, after George Whitefield came to America. It is rather the story of the Reverend Timothy Dwight, a story significant for the present day. After the Revolution there was a rise of infidelity. In 1794–1795, among the hundred-odd students at Yale not one in ten openly professed religion. The period between 1795 and 1802 has been regarded by many as the lowest ebb in Yale's religious history. But it has been shown that, beneath the surface, a considerable interest in morals and religion was going forward in students to whom the formal offices of religion were making little appeal. But President Dwight was the main force. His Christian influence touched every Yale man of that day. A servant of God, he was also an educator, fearless in intellectual combat.

> They [the infidels] thought the faculty were afraid of open discussion; but when they handed Dr. Dwight a list of subjects for class disputation, to their surprise he selected this: 'Is the Bible the word of God?' and told them to do their best. He heard all they had to say, answered them, and there was an end. He preached incessantly for six months on the subject, and all infidelity skulked and hid its head.[10]

Small wonder Dwight's effect did not end with the great revival of 1802 but went on through his quarter-of-a-century administration and into the later life of Yale. The well-known 'hall' that has housed the university's voluntary religious organizations over the years has very properly borne his name.

It is much the same story elsewhere — of higher learning called forth by Christian men. Though Princeton University had no official relationship with any synod, it was Presbyterian in its origin. Dartmouth College was the outgrowth of an Indian school founded out of missionary zeal by Eleazar Wheelock, a minister educated at Yale, who conceived of the new college as 'a voice . . . crying in the wilderness.' Columbia University, beginning as King's College, was founded by Episcopalians. On June 3, 1754, it was advertised by its president in the *New York Gazette:*

> The chief thing that is aimed at in this college is to teach and engage the children to know God in Jesus Christ, and to love and serve him, in all sobriety, godliness, and righteousness of life, with a perfect heart, and a willing mind; and to train them up in all virtuous habits, and all such useful knowledge as may render them creditable to their families and friends, ornaments to their country and useful to the public weal in their generations.

There was to be no sectarian pressure on any student, but an attempt 'to inculcate upon their tender minds, the great principles of Christianity and morality, in which true Christians of each denomination are generally agreed.' [11]

The University of Pennsylvania, under Benjamin Franklin's spirit, had no religious motive directly expressed in its beginning, though it can trace its origin to a charity school founded by the evangelist Whitefield. The constitution of the university has 'no mention of either religion or the church or the ministry. The foundation is human.

It was the largest human foundation which was laid for any college of America up to the middle of the eighteenth century.' Yet seven years after its founding the first provost named the Bible among the texts to be read — 'to be read daily from the beginning, to supply the deficiencies of the whole.' [12]

Under the influence of the Enlightenment and Thomas Jefferson, the University of Virginia favored no control of education by the Church. But even Jefferson never objected to religion on the campus. Hebrew, Latin, and Greek were to be taught, a room was appointed for religious services, and 'the professor of ethics was to deal with the proof of the being of God and the divine authority of morals.' [13] When later, in 1846, W. H. McGuffey joined the faculty, he introduced voluntary daily prayers — in reality not quite voluntary, perhaps, since he kept an album 'in which he recorded the name, home address, and denominational preference of every student who regularly attended his morning prayer services.' [14]

In the rest of the Old South, the religious motive in higher education was universal. Attendance at Sunday services was required and courses in religion were given regularly. On Sunday afternoon at the University of North Carolina students had to stand examination on the morning service, the Bible, or some course in religion. Public feeling against anything antireligious was strong, and agnostics could not be presidents or teachers in the state schools.[15]

No history of the religious influence in our higher education can forget the Christian motives that fired some of the great college presidents of the last century. Something of their feeling is conveyed in the belief of President Lord, of Dartmouth, that if a college lacks reverence for God

and practical regard for His laws, 'the influence of our
educated men will gradually undermine the fair fabric of
our national freedom and the ruins of our country will be
heaped up for an everlasting memorial, that neither liberty, nor learning, nor wealth, nor arts, nor arms, can stay
the decline of that people among whom the redeeming
spirit of Christianity has no permanent abode.' [16]

As America developed, religion continued on an even
greater scale to propagate education. All through the
opening West went the missionary influence of Princeton
and Yale, each termed 'the mother of colleges.' Between
1820 and 1860 twenty-five or more Church colleges arose
also in the Old South — their spirit bluntly expressed in
the inaugural address of D. H. Hill, professor of mathematics at Davidson, in 1855: 'A college without religious
instruction must necessarily be a public nuisance.' [17] Denominational rivalries only quickened the founding of colleges. A Georgia Baptist, hearing that Oglethorpe College
was about to be started by the Presbyterians, cried out:
'Shall it be said that six thousand Presbyterians built a
college at Midway and that forty thousand Baptists were
not able to build at Washington?' [18] The founding of the
207 colleges established before the War Between the
States that are in existence today — including 21 state
universities and 6 other public or semipublic institutions —
Donald Tewksbury [19] assigns to the following denominations: Presbyterian, 49; Methodist, 34; Baptist, 25; Con-
gregationalist, 21; Catholic, 14; Episcopal, 11; Lutheran,
6; Disciples, 5; German Reformed, 4; Universalist, 4;
Friends, 2; Unitarian, 2; Christian, 1; Dutch Reformed, 1;
United Brethren, 1.

Behind all higher education, of course, was a growing
public-school system in which, with the exception of a

development in Massachusetts and New York, the secular process had made no headway. As late as 1848, *Webster's Elementary Speller,* of which a million copies were sold each year, was 'outspoken in its religious character.' Indeed, 'no great educational leader before the Civil War would have denied that intellectual education was subordinate to religious values.' [20]

After the war the Churches increased their educational activity. The West, as New England before it, required not only a literate ministry, but the realization on the part of the Churches and benefactors that 'the peril of a new country is the peril of materialism' and that colleges under the Church were needed for 'the sake of the promotion of the higher civilization.' [21] Thus the great majority of all the colleges established in the nineteenth century were begun with a religious motive.

But what of the opposite of all this? What led to our time, when higher education is so frankly secular for the most part and much of its leading philosophy so naturalistic that some of the very language describing the role religion has played seems quaint and outmoded? What of the forces that caused colleges and universities founded in the Christian faith to slough off what they felt was an embarrassing relationship or at least keep only a polite speaking acquaintance with the Churches that fostered them?

There were many factors in this change, familiar to anybody who has thought even a little about education. The chief factor, of course, is the whole secular spirit that has pervaded our general life. It has had its influence from the beginning of our higher learning — in the latter part of the eighteenth century, when French freethinking affected America, and the moral and spiritual decline following the American Revolution touched campus life too.

For example, in the class of 1799 at Dartmouth, only one member was a professed Christian.²² The nineteenth century brought its own dose of Victorian rationalism and the shock of Darwinism, from which many churchmen ran like stricken deer.

But there were many factors in university life and structure itself that helped to reduce the place of religion. An appalling growth in size — not just in numbers educated, but in proliferation of plant and curriculum, struck heavy blows at liberal education concerned primarily with a sense of values and leading principles. The Morrill Land Grant Act of 1862 opened the way in every state and territory for the vast state universities. The new stress on research and scientific inquiry, the rising care for 'practical' and vocational subjects, general multiplication of aim and effort, and the rousing new interests that crowded into a wide variety of academic structures — all played their part. There was growing specialization in scholarship, specialization rich in its discoveries, productive of new knowledge, invaluable as a check on vagueness and bluffing, but 'so stunting to large-mindedness, so fatal to grasp on the whole truth which is the real truth.' ²³

Then there was the rise and spread of the system of free election of studies, for which President Eliot, of Harvard, was primarily responsible, though there were those before him who wanted it. Heavily influenced by the German universities and the Germanic conception of scholarship that still strongly affects our graduate schools, the elective system opened undergraduate education to a wide range of subjects, many of them fresh and valuable. But it further atomized and confused liberal education. It has deprived more than one American student of his cultural heritage, as colleges began to measure their quality by the thickness of their catalogues, and students, too young and inexperienced to know what the real choices were, jumped about joyously in the 'grasshopper' curriculum.

Chancellor Hutchins, who has at least had the felicity of accusing others as often as they have accused him, has never let President Eliot rest. 'Today,' he says, 'the young American comprehends only by accident the intellectual tradition of which he is a part and in which he must live: for its scattered and disjointed fragments are strewn from one end of the campus to the other. Our university graduates have far more information and far less understanding than in the colonial period.' [24]

In any academic program implying that one subject is as good and rewarding in humane terms as another is, a sense of values atrophies; and with a shrinking sense of values religion shrinks too. It becomes merely one thing among a lot of something else.

Religion suffered also from itself — from its own excess of sectarianism, from the low standards of education it condoned in some of its own colleges, from the snap courses in religion sometimes given for credit to those who needed academic mercy, from authoritarianism, from the bitter extremes of unreasonableness and lack of Christian or any other kind of charity reached in the Fundamentalist-Modernist controversy, from the spasms of the wild-eyed cults that were spawned off it, from the nervous obscurantism that was too often the Church's dusty answer to the new findings of science and research. The new state universities were not just politically afraid of religion out of overstrict fear of confounding Church and State; they were afraid of it because of the unlovely, small-minded spectacle the denominations so often presented, a travesty of their Lord and any truth that makes men noble and free. The cause of religion suffered also from the mistrust some Christians have always had of all higher learning in any form; from the persistent notion, for example, that 'any state university is a nest of godless sinners ' — a notion that tempts the wishful thinking of the presidents of Church colleges in the middle of a hard financial campaign. 'This caricature is, of course, as wide of the truth as the cartoon cherished by a few university professors, to the effect that churches are the eternal enemy of intellectual progress.' [25]

If, however, for many reasons over the years, religion has lost its place as 'the keystone of the educational arch,' [26] the last decade or so, particularly the period during and following the Second World War, has seen the reversal of tendencies in higher education that warred against it and the coming of fresh conceptions of liberal studies in which at least religion has the right and the duty to contend for its recognition. It is important to recognize what these conceptions arc.

For example, our new self-questioning higher education seeks once more some informing idea of man and his nature and the values he is born to serve. We arc no longer content with gadgets and superb equipment of all kinds, with tests and measurements that stop short of measuring or trying to measure really important things. There are dispositions in most colleges and universities toward less of our free-elective system and more of a simplified, integrated, and therefore more humane curriculum. All this does not mean a desire for narrow authoritarianism and rigid prescription. It is rather a desire that undergraduates have a chance — and they themselves have loudly demanded it — to have some acquaintance with the broad areas of knowledge and the experience of certain major disciplines. It is a desire, not for flimsy generalization, vast surveys of this and that, but for honest, careful work done in some perspective rather than the abject piling up of mere information. It is a desire to look again at the humane past and to restore to students their humane heritage, in the hope of helping them be more intelligent about the present and the future. All this is a reversal of the way education has been running in America for well over fifty years.

This new spirit has been marked, as it should be, by a breaking down of academic departmentalism and of narrow specialization. The old and often ignorant quarrel between the humanities and the natural and social sciences is less grim by far. The teachers of the humanities are seeing the rich place of the sciences and social studies, both as liberal disciplines and as steps to human betterment. And the scientists see the need of studies that deal with values that are the special province of arts and letters, of philosophy and history — and, some hope, religion.

There is a new faith that men can both conduct research and teach, each enterprise warming and informing the other; that they can see both the specific and the general, the living present in relation to the living past; and that, against a background of fearless inquiry and speculation, they can know something of the high hours of the imagination that complete our reason and form not the meanest portion of our lives as men. In short, the postwar world is demanding of education a great subject matter, handled with depth and breadth and fitted to really human ends — an education concerned with values. Any such education cannot escape the question of what place it should give or not give to religion. If education seriously seeks for meaning and significance, if it pretends to regard the

whole of human life, if it wants to be universal enough
to do the work of a ' university,' how can it avoid paying
attention to the Hebrew and Christian traditions and to
the present working of religion in men's lives? These are
the thoughts that give hope to Christians as they see how
things are running in higher learning just now.

Christians and everyone else eagerly looked forward to
what was generally regarded as the most important pro-
nouncement on higher education in our time. In the
spring of 1943, President Conant, of Harvard, appointed a
University Committee on the Objectives of a General Education in a Free Society. The Committee spent nearly
three years, with a budget of $60,000 and the widest kind
of consultation, looking at the problem of both school and
college education. They were concerned, not primarily
with any future course of study they might recommend
for Harvard, but with the country as a whole. The report
published in 1945 under the title, *General Education in a
Free Society,* ' though nominally addressing President
Conant,' was really addressed to ' the whole nation.' [27]

The Harvard Committee supports the trend we have already observed in postwar educational thought. Its plea
for ' general education ' stresses simply the term that ' is
now standard American for the older " Liberal Education," whose genteel connotations it discards.' [28] It wants
for the good and free citizen in a free society some common knowledge of the liberal and humane tradition. It
holds that ' a supreme need of American education is for
a unifying purpose and idea.' [29] It turns away from the ex-
cessive license of the free elective system and its uncritical
fragmentation of life. Though granting that this system
was ' necessary, even inevitable,' when President Eliot introduced it, the report observes the harm done through

the dissolving 'exuberance of freedom to which it led.'[30] It proposes a common core of studies for the four-year college, with grounding in the sciences, the social sciences, and the humanities. It puts importance on recovery of man's heritage and the past, one of the aims of education being 'to break the stranglehold of the present upon the mind.'[31] The abilities to be fostered in men and women by general education are, above all others, these four: '*to think effectively, to communicate thought, to make relevant judgments, to discriminate among values.*'[32] (The italics are those of the Report.)

To the friends of religion the Harvard Report was a major disappointment — so much so that, in our own judgment, they have missed its very important, though perhaps not intended, significance for their own cause. The tone of the document, of course, gives ground for their feeling. It is clearly humanistic and reflects no genuine concern for religion at all, though it has engaging references to it. It recognizes what democracy owes to faith — the ideals of human dignity and human duty to others drawing much upon 'the similarly interwoven commandments of the love of God and the love of neighbor.'[33] It carefully makes clear: 'We must perforce speak in purely humanistic terms, confining ourselves to the obligations of man to himself and to society. But we have been careful so to delimit humanism as not to exclude the religious ideal'[34] — a statement that calls up memories of John Dewey's zeal for 'religious attitudes,' though on other points of educational faith the authors of the Report are not to be confused with Mr. Dewey. And the faint praise given religion in another reference to democracy is in like vein: 'Education is not complete without moral guidance; and moral wisdom may be obtained from our religious heritage.' [35]

Actually, the Report cannot find easily the desired ' unifying purpose and idea ' the Committee feels is our sore need. It makes clear it is not in religion:

> Certainly, if the various fields of study do not represent a common discipline or give anything like a common view of life, then such unity as the college has must come chiefly from imponderable tradition or simple gregariousness.

> This, then, or something like this, is the present state: an enormous variety of aim and method among colleges as a whole and much the same variety on a smaller scale within any one college. This condition, which seemingly robs liberal education of any clear, coherent meaning, has for some time disturbed people and prompted a variety of solutions. Sectarian, particularly Roman Catholic, colleges have of course their solution, which was generally shared by American colleges until less than a century ago: namely, the conviction that Christianity gives meaning and ultimate unity to all parts of the curriculum, indeed to the whole life of the college. Yet this solution is out of the question in publicly supported colleges and is practically, if not legally, impossible in most others. Some think it the Achilles' heel of democracy that, by its very nature, it cannot foster general agreement on ultimates, and perhaps must foster the contrary. But whatever one's views, religion is not now for most colleges a practicable source of intellectual unity. [36]

If the unity of purpose in the search for *lux* and *veritas* arises from ' simple gregariousness,' and if the dignity of man springs, as the Report says it does, merely from our

'common humanity' — a concept not wholly humanistic,
since concession is made that such dignity is 'equally
compatible with a religious view of life' [37] — it would seem
that education ought to be at least gregarious enough to
include anything that has been significant for 'common
humanity,' which would by no means involve the extreme
license of the free-elective system. It has no such significance for the Harvard Committee:

> We are not at all unmindful of the importance of re-
> ligious belief in the completely good life. But, given the
> American scene with its varieties of faith and even of
> unfaith, we did not feel justified in proposing religious
> instruction as a part of the curriculum.[38]

By the same token, politics might be excluded because
there are Democrats and Republicans; physics, because
there are divergent views about cosmic rays; or athletics,
because some like Harvard and some like Yale. On this
theory, any matter lively enough to call forth more than
one deeply or widely held point of view is a doubtful item
in the curriculum. This seems very little like either 'simple
gregariousness' or 'the imponderable tradition' — or, for
that matter, free range of thought in a free society. The
friends of religion have ground for disappointment here,
and perhaps the friends of learning have too.

Harvard has done many fine things in the name of religion, and distinguished religious thought and action have
marked both many of its students and its faculty, even
though the present document, which mentions the educational value of participating in a glee club or an orchestra,
says nothing of the chapel or of Brooks House, long a center of religious and social service.[39] But Harvard 'has
often been reproached for indifference or infidelity concern-

ing religion.' [40] And a critic of our educational scene points out that in important official statements from the university and some of its officers there has been little ground to question such reproach.[41] At the Harvard Tercentenary in 1936 the place of religion on the programs was negligible: 'Among the sixty-two honorary degrees awarded to distinguished guests on that occasion, only two could be thought of as being related to their religious work.' [42] 'Enormous advances were recorded in every field of human endeavor except one.' [43]

Yet, looked at in another light, the Harvard Report should encourage, rather than depress, those who want religion to have a place in education. For the kind of college course the Report endorses — the quest for values, the common heritage, and abilities making for the good life of man — at least gives ground for asking with renewed fervor: 'How can religion be ruled out of all that?' And a careful distinction must, of course, be made. It is easy enough to follow Harvard's reasoning in dismissing religion as an over-all working principle or 'a practicable source of intellectual unity.' That simply proceeds from the Committee's judgment of religion or, perhaps more fairly, of our present secular society. But to offer religion no place at all as a part of a modern curriculum — that does not logically follow if one reads the Report with much of the sympathy and enthusiasm it so often inspires. For the document is asking for leading ideas and a quality in human life that religion, time out of mind, has notably fostered. Therefore, the Christian can hardly be blamed if he sees his own faith, not alien to, but actually the forming and completing agent of the kind of education Harvard describes in a treatise of such general distinction that it will be one of the landmarks in educational thought.

'The search continues,' the Report says, 'and must continue for some over-all logic, some strong, not easily broken frame within which both college and school may fulfill their at once diversifying and uniting tasks. This logic must be wide enough to embrace the actual richness and variegation of modern life.'[44] Well, religion surely is part of that richness and variety, and any logic of education should be wide enough to embrace it. Moreover, if, as the Report says, 'to study either past or present is to confront, in some form or another, the philosophic and religious fact of man in history,'[45] and if, as it says also, 'Western culture may be compared to a lake fed by the streams of Hellenism, Christianity, science, and democracy,'[46] what cultural perspective naturally follows and how can right education diminish it?

But the heart of the Report, for any Christian who reads it, lies in its stress on two of the four abilities to be nourished by general education — the ability to make relevant judgments and the ability to discriminate among values. The first 'involves the ability of the student to bring to bear the *whole range* of ideas [italics mine] upon the area of experience.'[47] The second demands 'not only awareness of different kinds of value but of their relations,'[48] 'not just knowledge of values but commitment to them'[49] — at which point the Committee has a sense of the country into which it has strayed and significantly cautions the reader that it is not suggesting the turning of a school or college into a reform school or a church.[50] Then comes this later passage:

The ideal of free inquiry is a precious heritage of Western culture; yet a measure of firm belief is surely part of the good life. A free society means toleration,

which in turn comes from openness of mind. But freedom also presupposes conviction; a free choice — unless
it be wholly arbitrary (and then it would not be free)
— comes from belief and ultimately from principle. . . .

A measure of belief is necessary in order to preserve
the quality of the open mind. If toleration is not to become nihilism, if conviction is not to become dogma-
tism, if criticism is not to become cynicism, each must
have something of the other.[51]

If the desired result of education is thus really reflective
commitment and the choice of values that govern life,
how can one possibly choose if he be left ignorant of what
one of the great choices can be? The Harvard Report
seemingly shares President Conant's own conviction that
'unless the educational process includes *at each level of
maturity* some continuing contact with those fields in
which value judgments are of prime importance, it must
fall far short of the ideal.' [52] If so, are not college men and
women mature enough, at their level, to deal with religion
as part of their heritage, even though there be divers notions and opinions of what it is? If choice is the important
thing for them, why not really let them choose? They de-
serve that chance, and in the great bulk of higher education in America they are not getting it. They need it to
help complete the bearing of what is noblest and most
human in Harvard's own report.

One of the shrewdest and most winning sentences in
the whole Harvard document is this: 'When logic and
apparent fact fall out with one another, the scientist takes
the fact and leaves the logic for future repair.' [53] Not only
scientists — we all do it at times, because we are human
and susceptible to surrounding climates of opinion. Even

committees are tempted to do it, subject to the forms and pressures of the time. Could it be that Harvard has accepted the prevailing fact of secularism and left some of the logic of its own position for future repair? Surely it already says enough to leave wide open, and to bring forward for new discussion, the place of religion in the kind of education the Report so sincerely tells us can be ours in our time.

It would be a mistake, however, to think the Harvard Report a mirror of what many other colleges and universities are saying and doing about religion. As we have noted, it does not even reflect the present religious life of Harvard itself. Actually, students and educators the country over are asking that something be done. They are aware of the widespread religious illiteracy that is a block to learning even in other fields; and they know the deeper need of some high values and convictions. As early as 1941, Dean Charles W. Gilkey reported to the bicentennial conference at the University of Pennsylvania: ' It is my definite impression that there have been greater changes during the last five years in the attitude of the present student generation toward religion, as compared with its immediate predecessor, than during any other similar period in the forty years of my own observation.' [54] Recent surveys of college students and their thinking show a continuing and mounting interest in religious thought. Three years before Dean Gilkey's remark, the president of Yale University had said: ' I call on all members of the faculty, as members of a thinking body, freely to recognize the tremendous validity and power of the teaching of Christ in our life-and-death struggle against the forces of selfish materialism. If we lose that struggle, judging from present events abroad, scholarship as well as religion will disappear.' [55] And in 1940, President Dodds, looking forward to Princeton's new professorship of Religious Thought (now developed into a five-man department of Religion), told his trustees: 'Princeton's historic position, its present conviction, and the acute needs of the time demand that we take vigorous steps to meet our responsibility. We must develop in our students a fuller understanding of religion and its significance.' [56]

A full account of what has actually happened on our college and university campuses since 1900 is admirably given in Professor Merrimon Cuninggim's book *The College Seeks Religion*.[57] It is an impressive story, one that may well surprise even the friends of religion. Professor Cuninggim shows the scope of religious life and thought in academic life — both that of voluntary organizations and that of institutional support in or outside the curriculum. The Christian Associations, the Student Volunteer Movement, the Church-sponsored religious organizations, the university chaplains, directors of religious work, deans of chapels, and the work of various councils and foundations (the Religious Education Association, founded in 1903; the National Council on Religion in Higher Education, which has greatly raised the standard of personnel in the teaching of religion; the Hazen Foundation and the Danforth Foundation), all form a wide and effective activity. The book traces also the rise of actual instruction in religion as part of the curriculum.

All this activity and curricular development impresses Professor Cuninggim, but it does not deceive him. To be sure, the thesis of his book is 'that the secularization of higher education seems to have reached its peak around the time of the First World War, and that since then the colleges have recaptured much of their lost concern for the religious development of their students and have increasingly assumed responsibility for such nurture.' [58] He sees religion gradually moving into a central place in higher education. But he is, at the same time, a frank and careful enough critic to admit that the spirit of secularism, though arrested, ' has continued to be characteristic of the collegiate scene ' [59] and ' that the majority of student bodies is still composed of happy pagans who are blissfully ignorant in the field.' [60] The atmosphere of most American education is not ' sympathetic to the development of a high religion in students ' and does not ' encourage undergraduates to discover religious insights, to adopt religious patterns of living, and withal to do so with the conscious realization that it is religion they find and follow.' [61]

In 1945–1946 a series of faculty consultations on religion in higher education was held under the auspices of three national foundations and councils. [62] Sixteen well-known and respected scholars, at the invitation of administrators and faculty committees — there were far more invitations than could be accepted — had fairly leisurely and detailed discussions with the faculties of fifty-three colleges and universities. The consultants felt that ' in many institutions the majority of the faculty with whom they talked are either hostile to or indifferent toward religion.' [63]

As to faculty members, the consultants are surprised more often than they should have been at their naïveté in religious matters. Both those who declared themselves ' hostile ' or ' neutral ' to religion revealed the most archaic and regressive notions about the contemporary religious situation and the intellectual temper of modern liberal Christianity and Judaism. Most of them seem to rely on garbled childhood memories to tell them what religion is and their familiarity with the literature and living spokesmen of liberal religion was strangely scant for cultivated and intelligent people. Occasionally faculty members denounced religion as 'superstition,' 'pre-scientific benightedness,' and 'an emotional crutch,' 'both useless and dangerous.' A larger group were convinced that a humanistic or naturalistic creed was wholly adequate for a modern man.[64]

But the consultants felt, even so, that 'there are signs in many quarters, some of them the most unexpected, that the place of religion is due for re-examination.'[65] They sensed 'real vitality, intellectual and moral, in American colleges.' They came to feel that 'what is chiefly needed is that the case for religion be given a fair hearing in the open forum of academic discussion.'[66] They would agree that 'in the deepest sense the problem of the meaningful inclusion of religion is not drawing to a close; rather, it has just begun.'[67] At the heart of that problem is the task of first seeing exactly what the relations of religion and liberal education are.

CHAPTER

3

LIBERAL EDUCATION AND RELIGION

IT IS A PITY that 'liberal education' still implies what it does to so many people. They think it something chilly and remote from all common concern. Our new habit of saying 'general' instead of 'liberal' comes of a democratic and well-intended desire to renounce the snobberies the older term even yet widely suggests. But something has been lost in this transaction. The word 'liberal,' when rightly understood, has strength and meaning — and real implications for democracy — that the word 'general' does not have at all. We trust, anyhow, that the reader of this book has long ago cleared his mind of the notion that liberal education is the polite learning — or the lack of any learning, as it often was — carefully reserved only for the sons of well-to-do gentlemen. We hope it means something more even than the preprofessional period assigned to doctors, lawyers, preachers, teachers, monks, and dentists. For liberal education, once the education of those who were not slaves or bondsmen, in the political sense, has now become the education of those who would be free men in quite another sense. It is designed, at its best, for anyone who would leave the slavery of ignorance for the freedom conferred by knowledge

— who would be thus 'liberated' from servility to prejudice, passion, a vocation, or any rut of any kind that limits and shrinks the human spirit. No longer, in America at least, is it a privilege granted by birth alone. And we are doing our best to remove the economic barriers that would deny it to any person who really wants it and is capable of taking advantage of it. In the middle of the century liberal education has become the education of free citizens. Thus it is the concern of all thinking people.

Any educator finds it both amusing and a little sad to see how thoughts on higher education are supposed to be 'professional' thoughts, left to professors, deans, and presidents who presumably have the advantage of some occult powers and a whole hatful of professional jargon. Actually, liberal education concerns deeply elemental things and has never been the monopoly of colleges and universities. Men and women without number have acquired genuinely liberal educations by their own effort. Out of some depth and range of their own, by natural aptitude or hard work, they have made themselves the superior of many a bachelor of arts and even some doctors of philosophy, in the quantity and quality of what they read, in their ability to think and express their thought, in the play of their imagination, and in the scope of their informed sympathies. They should sober any educator. Colleges can learn much, if they will, by studying some truly cultivated men and women who are not their alumni.

For most of us, however, a college or a university is still the likeliest means to a liberal education. And the conviction rises everywhere, both in school and out, that free, responsible citizens, the products of good liberal education, are an increasing need. What colleges do or fail to do, therefore, becomes the serious affair, not just of educators,

but of the whole community. And anyone human has both
the instinct and the means of being interested in the human
questions that are the staple inquiry of liberal education:
Who am I? Where do I really live? What do I want in
life and what should I want? How can I best do what I
ought to do and what will it mean if I do it? What can I
do and think about when I'm not at work? What have the
best things been? How can I share in these — out of the
past and the present? What faith controls and informs my
life? What and whom do I hope for, love, and serve?
These are the questions raised by liberal education because they are the questions raised by life itself. They are
plain and mysterious, as life is, but alien to no one. All
men must ignore them or try to answer them.

Both the academic and nonacademic reader can see by
this time where we are in our general inquiry. We are on
the ground of dispute as to how far a liberal education
can include religion and remain liberal or how far it can
be liberal and exclude religion. Thus far we have not
tried to conceal our hope of showing that liberal education itself creates the need for the examination of religion and religious values — that, in addition, it creates in
thinking people a desire to weigh religious knowledge and
gives them a kind of capability for doing so. We now ap-
proach more closely the thesis we have suggested in earlier pages: a liberal education that omits religion is not, in
the nature of things, liberal education at all.

In doing this we run straight into a countercharge. Religion and liberal studies, it is said, simply do not mix.
The religion that conceivably, since it is a large part of
life and history, might have a logical place in university
study, would destroy, paradoxically, the liberal character
of the liberal education it might otherwise complete.

What have revelation, a suprahuman order, commitment to a divine power, and all the earthly dynamite implicit in the love of God — what have these enormous prejudices and persuasions to do with the impersonal quest for truth, objective investigation, scientific procedure, and the whole climate of a higher education that, above all else, must start with no assumptions? Must the dispassionate calm of library and laboratory feel the hot breath of the sects, the fervor of intrenched bigotry and superstition? What has Athens to do with Jerusalem?

Let us first recall what liberal education now seems to be and the new emphases placed on some of the benefits it offers men and women. Its ideal is a high human product, obtained just frequently enough in actual life to make us not despair of an education wise and bold enough to seek creating it.

Liberal education looks toward a man who knows how to think, how to express his thought, and how to receive the thoughts of others. He can follow the lights and shadows of a printed page, knowing what is main and what is subordinate. He is less an 'educated' man than, as one wise person suggested, 'a potentially educated'[1] one, having both a fair estimate of his own ignorance and, at the same moment, of those chief techniques and methods of acquiring new knowledge that will lessen his ignorance as time goes by and afford him ways of continuing his liberal education until the day he dies. If fortunate, he has penetrated into at least one field of learning — not necessarily or even preferably the field of his future career — sufficiently to know what learning is. His education has, with luck, not been merely descriptive. It has been more than walks through museums, notes on lectures, or even the reading of great books, though all these will help him.

Somewhere he has dug in and had some real adventure of his own.

Yet the liberally educated man has learned perspective also. He has some knowledge of the natural world. He knows the scientist's breadth and precision, as well as some basic truths about the society in which he lives. Music, art, literature, history, and philosophy are not to him merely means of 'escape' or unnecessary appendages to reality, but the source of high values for his own choosing, values given attraction and power by the excellent forms in which they were expressed. Out of new values attained and older values refined, he knows new obligations for himself, new disciplines for his life, some creative renunciations. Principles persist for him beyond the shifting data of existence and abide in spite of the fashions of the world. There is an island within himself, an 'inward endowment' and resource that is beyond the fortunes of business and politics. He draws on the humane past and thus lives a life antecedent to his birth. He may even know a language other than his own, one in which he does not have to do his worrying. Reasons and facts mean more to him than propaganda. But beyond the coolness of his reason he senses a realm of the imagination and an invitation to sympathies, causes, loyalties, and reflective commitments. He feels his debt to others and the worth and dignity of other men out of those things which have possessed his own mind and heart.

And he would have humor enough to smile at anyone who would attribute all these qualities to him. For he would know that art is long and time is short and human nature a very complicated business. That would be not the least part of his liberal education.

This high ideal of human life, this 'acquired illumination' as Newman called it, is real and attractive enough to men so that they have sacrificed, as their fathers and mothers have sacrificed for them, that something of it might be theirs. They have put off things dear to their immediate desires, postponed learning the tricks of some trade, that they might have a chance at an education which would really make them free — free for work and leisure, for being something as well as doing something. The sons of dentists and lawyers and businessmen have tried to be something else before they in turn became dentists and lawyers and businessmen. And their fathers have blessed them, out of an intimation of 'some knowledge worth possession for what it is, and not merely for what it does.' For liberal education is no sleek adventure in shrewdness and mere self-interest. It has one superb object above all others — to open the mind and heart, under law, to the highest excellence and most significant life possible to man.

We are coming to see, moreover, the relevance of liberal education to practical life. It can and should be used. It is hard to realize now that a hundred years ago in the cathedral at Oxford the divine giving the sermon of the day could set forth these twofold advantages of a classical education: 'it enables us to look down with contempt on those who have not shared its advantages, and also fits us for places of emolument not only in this world, but in that which is to come.' The use of liberal studies today is, one trusts, more humane. But they do give even a vocational help to a man or woman. Businessmen more and more realize this. The head of a well-known industrial plant said to some of us not long ago: 'We look for men to come into our business, and too often all we can find are technicians. We want men who are *more* than technicians.' As President Dodds, of Princeton, has pointed out, the mind trained in associative thinking, applying the experience and methods of one field to the problems of another, integrating humanistic and scientific knowledge, and carrying on its own self-education after college, is a clear vocational asset. 'It will help its owner to a successful career, and it is scholastic snobbishness to insist that nothing useful should be studied in college.'[2] The 'useful' does not mean the narrowly vocational, nor does this view gainsay the point Newman made so persuasively — that liberal knowledge is its own end and reward. But President Dodds sees, as indeed Newman saw too, the fuller implication of liberal education for the responsible worker and citizen:

There are two sides to a college education, and partisans of one are apt to depreciate the other. One is preparation for one's own personal happiness by enlarging one's world of ideas and by developing subjective appreciation of art, literature, history, and science. An education should enable a man to get more fun out of life, by giving him access to the broad empire of the mind where he can find a recuperative release from the restrictions of the work-a-day world. It is the life of the mind and the soul that sustains one in defeat and gives meaning to victory. But education misses the mark if it contributes only to one's own pleasure, no matter what level that pleasure attains. The danger is that the intellectual person, concentrating upon the inward look, will yield to the temptation to become merely an observer, good at protesting but poor in constructive attainment. If the educated person is a self-centered person, proud of his inflexible principles, opinionated and introspective, he will seek to avoid the citizen's responsibility for getting things done and to escape his share of the world's work.[3]

There are many kinds of colleges and universities, and they will vary greatly in both the degree and quality of liberal education they can include in their programs. But almost everywhere, especially in the technical schools, there is a new awareness of the need for liberal studies. Particularly noteworthy is the demand coming from students themselves for a broader view of life and a more humane preparation for it. They are weary — the more thoughtful of them — of developing unrelated specialties and of learning all kinds of bright tricks without any over-all meaning or purpose. Some of us have been asked specifically if we could not work, as educators, for a course of study that would at least raise early in the curriculum some of the questions worthy to be asked by man. 'The answers,' the students say, 'are harder, of course, and quite another matter. But we'd like some sense of the implication of things. We are tired of heaped-up fragments. All this is our right as men.' It would seem a fair request.

These students are bright enough and direct enough, moreover, to see that the real questions in liberal education cannot be raised without involving philosophy and religion. Many of them are pagans tempered by experience — 'reluctant pagans,' Professor Cuninggim has called them. Many of them have no use for organized religion as they have seen it practiced and set forth in the churches. Many of them are stuck deep in the secularism of their time. But when they tell you what is really on their minds, you can see their dissatisfaction with their own vacuity of belief, their desire to come to some conviction, whatever that conviction may be. They at least want grounds for rejecting what they reject. They want their liberal education to be comprehensive enough to give them some of that ground.

One cannot reflect on the nature of liberal studies and this new demand for them without seeing two things. First, these studies create a disposition to extend one's intellectual quest to include religion; and, secondly, religion can, when it is not narrow and provincial, powerfully augment the desire for liberal education. It conceives of all man does as a ' calling ' and of all life as a piece, a unity of richly component parts. It cannot contemplate with pleasure the fragmentation of human beings or the life of the tangent.

True religion does more, however, than merely create a disposition toward liberal education. It makes an important contribution to the actual body of such studies. Three great cultures — the Greek, the Roman, and the Hebrew — have formed the Western world. Why should a college man or woman be ignorant of one of the three? One cannot penetrate into art, architecture, music, literature, history, social thought, or philosophy without the passport of some real knowledge of the Bible and the great religious writings both in and out of the Church. These subjects are so thoroughly shot through with religious allusions and concepts that they cannot be understood by religious illiterates. Indeed, one of the poverties of our contemporary mind is our ignorance of the common symbols that have expressed great ideas. Slowly the secular books, even, have been closing to those who cannot understand the symbols these books have been using for nineteen hundred years. What futility in our revived effort at recovering the heritage of our past if we refuse to look at whole pages in one of its most vital records! We are avid lovers of public opinion, but we stupidly ignore some of the best public opinion ever given to us on what really matters to the mind and heart.

Man's whole intellectual history is a shorn story without the knowledge of his quest for religious faith. His social institutions are imperfectly understood apart from the role religion has played — for good and for ill — in their strength and weaknesses. In his increasing love of self-analysis, his exploration into the subtlest recesses of his own nature, how can man analyze, without regarding the place of belief and conviction, the problem of adequate focus and attachment, in the psychic play and interplay of his own being and in the tensions that his mind and body know?

There is a kind of paradox in America's deepening religious ignorance. As a recent convention of the American Council on Education noted, there is no marked difference in the religious concept of the average pupil in the eighth grade of school and the average college graduate. And the paradox is this: in colonial days, when only five per cent of the population was actively identified with the Church, religion and education were in close co-operation. 'Today more than half of the people in this country report church affiliation. And yet, with half of the population going through the motions of being church members and actively concerned with religion and its spiritual emphasis on their lives, there are practically no working relations between education and religion.' [4] President Butler, of Columbia, once said that our growing lack of knowledge of the Bible and Shakespeare — though Shakespeare has had a great deal of help lately — was bringing about a new variety of the Dark Ages. The new religious ignorance can be as hard a blow to liberal education as it can to religion itself.

What blocks, then, the inclusion of religion in liberal studies? Why the scant academic account of Christianity in a land so widely confessed to be Christian? As much as anything else the barrier is the cult of 'objectivity.' This is itself, of course, but one phase of our secularism. In its name much is done and not done on a modern campus, and religion is omitted from serious consideration. For religion is regarded as a 'packed' matter, full of assumptions, drenched with emotion, atomized in itself by the contending sects. Its history is the history of authority, of compromises with worldly power and chicanery, of centuries given over to bitter schisms and religious wars rather than to any calm analysis. It has bred saints and fanatics rather than philosophers and scientists and unbiased thinkers. It closes the mind very early, out of habits of devotion and commitment begun in youth. It lacks the open-mindedness of the impersonal quest for truth — in brief, the 'objectivity' required for liberal study.

With the fearless pursuit of truth no one can quarrel. The thinking portion of mankind has never blessed that member of the House of Commons who remarked long ago, ' That a thing is an anomaly I consider to be no objection to it whatever.' [5] The great English critic to whom that remark was unfortunately made has given us a better view of what we mean by living by ideas. It is this:

> When one side of a question has long had your earnest support, when all your feelings are engaged, when you hear all round you no language but one, when your party talks this language like a steam-engine and can

imagine no other, — still to be able to think, still to be irresistibly carried, if so it be, by the current of thought to the opposite side of the question, and, like Balaam, to be unable to speak anything *but what the Lord has put in your mouth.* I know nothing more striking, and I must add that I know nothing more un-English.[6]

Beyond the critic's impersonal thought is also the scientist's impersonal obligation to keep pressing for all possible data. He must beware of all presuppositions. One remembers how John Hunter, the great eighteenth century physician and anatomist, rebuked his students for theories and conclusions based on inadequate research: 'Don't think; try and be patient.' Our regard for the fact around the corner, for the merciless pursuit of what may be embarrassing evidence — this trait does us honor. And now, when we have seen whole nations put down the free play of the mind, their scholarship in slavery to dictators and factions, we should care more than ever to preserve the mind from bondage of any kind.

But the cult of 'objectivity' has jumped the track. It has become more than the honest pursuit of truth. It has become almost a religion itself and has raised in the modern mind a new kind of god — a god in whose name we can bewitch ourselves. In a world shining with equipment for research, where there is a 'recognized authority' in almost every field waiting to bristle at anything that has not consulted him, where every thought, however small, must be checked and double-checked, where the height to which knowledge has come and the depth to which it is still unsounded must sober any modest mind, the cult of 'objectivity' has a singular power and attraction. And it has abused its power.

There is a rising suspicion among us that the cult of 'objectivity' isn't the cool, bloodless thing it is thought to be. It is perhaps not wholly unspotted from the world. This suspicion is a very healthy development in our recent thinking. Indeed, men have begun to wonder if some totalitarian enslavements of the mind were not made possible by accumulated 'objective' indifference to high values and to high passions — if 'objectivity' did not take itself a captive. The treason of the scholar has been, not his failure to maintain his mind, but his abject surrender of the best his mind told him — his ignoble reticence, his detachment from any high commitment born of his reflection, his refusal to serve and fight for loyalties his own pursuit of truth must at moments have given him. Refusing to be a committed man, he allowed himself to be an uncommitted child. He was ripe for the plucking by any committed brute that came along. 'The desire to avoid controversy in the highest matters is a sure sign of failing faith and nerve — a kind of pernicious anaemia of the spirit. What better preparation for tyranny and mass-manipulation than this emptying the soul of all that gives it its real and individual power and quality?' [7]

But even where 'objectivity' is still free, where it has been fought for and assiduously preserved by those who held some values were settled beyond all mistake, is it really what it has been cracked up to be? Is 'objectivity' really objective? Does it not actually start with the presupposition that scholarship is or can be divorced from all personal background? One who thinks so is probably self-deceived or merely lying. The most devoted attempt at reasoning suffers from the necessary selection and abstraction it must perform, from the state of the man, the time, and the place in which the reasoning occurs. 'Liberal

rationalism' has a blithe disregard of the conditions life
constantly puts on all our thought just as it has also a contempt for the possibility of what Professor Tillich has
called the prime 'Unconditioned,' on which everything,
including reason itself, might well depend. The conception
of reason as an impeccable judge holding antiseptic court
in a vacuum is a wilder kind of wishful thinking than that
religion is so often accused of. Priding themselves on being free from any authority but that of truth, and therefore being open to truth from any source, the 'liberal
rationalists' feel themselves bound to neutrality and impartiality in the conflict of ideas. Though they have not
lived up to it, their self-confessed task is the presenting of
all varieties of belief and unbelief as objectively as possible. The student is supposed to think and then make up
his mind. The assumption is that, if 'there be free competition of all ideas and ideals, the truth will receive the ap-
proval of reason and error will be cast out.' What this
assumption forgets is that 'the competition of truth with
error will lead to the victory of truth only when the desire
for truth is stronger than other desires. . . . When con-
fronted by the intellectual and moral failure of many who
have enjoyed a liberal education, it can only reassert its
faith in the supremacy of reason and seek for more facts
and better methods of imparting them.' [8]

To say all this is not to depreciate reason itself. It has
delivered us from errors and superstitions without number. It has helped religion to some of its best discoveries
about itself. It has proffered the ground on which science
can occur and given science its necessary factor, the reasoning observer. But when rationalism refuses to see what
is so often thwarting it, when it refuses to see the conditions life does put on our thought, when it dogmatically

closes its mind to the possibility of experience transcending its earth-bound and often pride-ridden view — then
reason has placed itself beyond its own capacity for criticism. Reason then is no longer reasonable about itself.

True 'objectivity,' the reasonable life of reason, consists in no such naïveté or pride about its own absolute
power. It consists rather in knowing the obstacles in human nature that reason itself must confront, in being more
eager than ever to summon all experience and thought for
making up a judgment, in concealing no fact we do not
like, in really trying to see from all points of view. Merely
because 'objective' thinking is not the sterilized essence
it frequently poses to be, we need not 'lapse into nihilism
or scepticism. We must simply be more in earnest with
what we already recognise to be good habits: modesty,
self-criticism, and readiness to listen to one another. But
some of us must drop the exaggerated fear of making mis-
takes (or of being found out in them?) which leads us to
play safe by avoiding controversial questions and broad
inductions. This is the wrong kind of self-criticism, based
on the wrong kind of pride, and it impairs our value as
scholars and as teachers.' [9]

The cult of 'objectivity' arises, however, from more
than just the worship of reason. It includes the believers in
'naturalism,' who hold observable data as the exclusive
means to truth. One of the ablest of these, a man of great
gifts and one who has fought in many good causes, has
defined the 'naturalist' faith:

Naturalists assert that all powers, qualities and feelings attributable to man are contingent upon the existence of certain organic structures, and that there is no
evidence for the existence of disembodied spirit. They

wholeheartedly recognize the presence of the distinctively human qualities manifested in experience, and seek by wise control of causes and consequences ' to turn the friction of material forces into the light of ideal goods.' [10]

The 'naturalists' have a large hold on American education and perhaps give it its ' underlying and pervading philosophy.' [11] Many of them, as does the statement just given, with its quotation from Santayana, take on a humanistic tinge and ideals rubbed up out of the friction of material forces.

The naturalists, like all ' objective ' thinkers, deplore an assumption. Their dismissal of religion and its values arises from their dread of religious presuppositions. But their restriction of the search for truth to their method alone involves a dogma that is really very startling. As Dr. George Buttrick has astutely observed, ' One of the sorriest assumptions of secular education is its assumption that it makes no assumptions.' [12] Actually it makes one whacking assumption — that all life is secular.

The prevailing shibboleth of ' objectivity ' has not gained its currency, however, just out of intellectual positions consciously taken by those who serve it as an ideal. It is a convenient catchword for those who are content to confine their intellectual activity to their own specialty, who have no desire or energy for breaking out of departmental boundaries. Pascal pointed out long ago that being busy is one way to avoid the misery of thinking. American academic life is full of men and women who are quite content to stay within the enchantment of their own activity. They have no impulse for pursuing larger meanings, or often even the meaning of their own specialty. Hundreds of

thousands of college graduates and college students —
who owe them much — can also testify that this is so.

To say this is not to discredit what these scholars and
teachers do. Nor is it to treat lightly the great men who
have been agnostics out of their sense of how much there
is to know, how many data are yet to come, how imperfect
our human comprehension is. On the ultimates of life they
see only a reserved judgment, one they will never make
in their own brief time. But there are others who have not
fairly earned the right to say, at least with any merit, 'I
have an open mind.' It is, for that matter, amusing to see
how quickly one can acquire in academic circles a kind of
reputation for profundity, modesty, and a gigantic intellect merely by refusing to conclude anything. But sometimes when these credits for 'open and fresh intelligence'
are passed out to those who have not really earned them,
it is useful, though never kind, to recall Bernard Shaw's
comment on Robert de Baudricourt that age cannot wither
him because he has never bloomed.

For there is another side to the 'open mind.' There is
such a thing as shying off from speculation, from the pursuit beyond our own rut of some real faith and philosophy
of life, not because we are careful and profound thinkers,
but because we choose not to think at all. We are too
timid, too lazy, too preoccupied, too blocked out by some
trap door that snapped shut early in our lives, to carry on
any real quest of truth. We become quite willing to manip-
ulate tiny gadgets and ideas, as long as enough goes on
adding up in a small way. The adventure dies in our own
spirits. We are content with fact piled on fact, with little
logical truths holding on, as Carlyle says, to one another's
skirts. We fall victim to a false 'scientism' — never held
by first-rate scientists — which assumes that apart from

science there is no other aspect of the world.* The true scientists have always recognized that they are merely ' selecting from experience *only* that which serves their scientific purpose and that their selection does not invalidate the unselected.' [13] Or with the aesthete we can shrink truth to a fleeting glimpse of beauty; or with the ' realist ' we can concentrate on ugliness and horror, his morbid preoccupation being but a striking aspect of our contemporary flight from meaning. To anyone so engrossed or so restricted, a small kind of clarity is easily possible. He resents all hint of larger questions and larger values as a troubling of his peace and concentration. If all he has is a ' chaos of clear ideas,' as someone once called Voltaire's fifty-five volumes, or if he has but one idea, he can easily allow that to become more congenial to him than a cosmos which would cost him prodigious inconvenience and all

---

* ' It is undoubtedly true that a very large proportion of present-day students of the natural sciences (and these, as has been said, form a very large proportion of the total population of our universities) attempt to live by the light of their scientific knowledge alone. Behind this attempt lies the assumption, explicit or unconfessed, that no other light is available to them, that no reliable kind of knowledge exists except that which comes by their own technique of observation and experiment. Yet it is to be noticed that science itself can in the nature of the case give them no right to make this assumption. The knowledge that scientific knowledge is the only knowledge is not itself part of scientific knowledge; nor would its disappearance from the scientist's mind in any way affect the validity of any strictly scientific conclusion. Obviously the assumption that there is no other kind of knowledge than the scientific cannot itself be either proved or disproved by starting from purely scientific premises; the attempt to do either would involve a circular argument. Science itself is therefore one thing, while the elevation of science as the only source of human enlightenment is quite another thing — it is a dogma of modern secularism.' — John Baillie, *The Mind of the Modern University*, pp. 23–24, University Pamphlets, No. 1, S.C.M. Press, Ltd., London, 1946.

manner of strange intellectual work. Though he would scorn any other form of monasticism, he enters his own monastery — every university has a rich variety of such cells — and takes refuge in the cult of 'objectivity.' It is a perfect rest home for the mind.

The cult of 'objectivity' does not wholly rest, however. Beyond its own very legitimate scholarly endeavor, it loses its 'objectivity' in what should seem to its members a very alarming fashion. It takes many a pot shot, for example, at matters it has ruled outside its province. The sniping is often well covered and consists more in *obiter dicta* than in direct argument. The polite and seemingly 'objective' attitude toward religion one encounters on many a campus reminds one now and then of Dr. Flexner's story of the captain in Lord Nelson's navy who said, 'My lord, I have no prejudices, but God knows I hate a Frenchman.' Who does not remember the uninformed remarks on Christianity, the archaic conception of Biblical scholarship, he has heard tossed off gratuitously and sidewise by men learned in their own fields but not in this one? They make a caricature of what they do not know. Worse yet, in terms of 'objectivity' they show a disregard for primary sources — a failure to become acquainted with the great documents in Judaism and Christianity, let alone modern research in these fields — that they would despise if it were directed at any other field of learning.

Whatever else, intelligent Christianity is not a concealed religion. Its main tenets are very clear and its conception of human life very knowable, in spite of the confusing quarrels of all the sects and the differences of theologians. Its great themes stand in plain perspective. The documents on which it rests can be studied by anyone caring to examine them, the reasoning that supports it can be checked, the life that validates it in experience can be led.

This point was appreciated not long ago by one of the clearest-headed of American critics, Lionel Trilling, reviewing a book on religious trends in English poetry of the romantic movement. He notes that the author, who had published two earlier books in his series, writes from an avowed religious position:

> He remarks in his preface that some critics of the preceding two volumes have felt that his treatment of the subject has been distorted by the definiteness of his personal religious views. To this he replies that ' a study in the history of ideas by a man who has no ideas of his own would be neither very interesting nor very fruitful,' and the answer is a proper one.
>
> We can never hope for the complete absence of distortion in history or in criticism, and we must be grateful to the historian or the critic who lets us know just what his principle of relative distortion is. And a frank, reasoned, and openly aggressive religious commitment is a good deal more comfortable to deal with than the dim ' objectivity ' of many academic writers.[14]

The concealed religions are very common on the American campus. Sometimes they emerge and declare themselves, but very frequently they enjoy neither clear statement nor the opportunity of direct examination. John Henry Newman saw long ago that when theology is not taught, ' its province will not simply be neglected but will be actually usurped by other sciences, which will teach, without warrant, conclusions of their own in a subject-matter which needs its own proper principles for its due formation and disposition.'[15] Mankind is incurably religious and is always moving something forward, however vaguely and unconsciously, into the role of a faith. Stuart Sherman, who was close to academic life, saw this very keenly: ' Destroy a man's faith in God and he will worship humanity; destroy his faith in humanity and he will worship science; destroy his faith in science and he will worship himself; destroy his faith in himself and he will worship Samuel Butler.' [16]

Some of the hidden religions we have already noticed — the faiths of ' liberal rationalism,' naturalism, and ' scientism,' with their persistent yet often unrealized extensions or ' extra-beliefs.' There are many more. All subjects that touch man's life at all deeply or involve the making of judgments are full of them. A teacher brings the flavor of his own self to what he teaches, however impartial he may try to be in presenting all possible views on the matter at hand. His own twist and preference will, if openly expressed, do little harm. No good man expects another good man to be neutral on important issues. Moreover, students are less docile than we often think — indeed, there are cynics who hold that the best way to secure undergraduate acceptance of a point is to have some professor stoutly deny it. Unfortunately, the issue is not always openly declared, and there real harm is done. Some of the purest poisons ever brewed in a college classroom have been brewed without the realization of any but the most aware.

All this too has its ironical aspect. A teacher can set forth, with some sympathy and enthusiasm, a materialistic philosophy in many a field of learning — some poet of negation and his lyrical rapture over zero; the decadent art and thought of some perverted genius — all this to be sucked up as gospel or rejected, according to the wit and taste of the student. But almost never is it questioned as regards its academic propriety. One of the most eloquent disquisitions some of us ever heard in a lecture hall was that given to a view of deity as some dim form of world mind coming slowly to consciousness, refined gradually by pity at human suffering, the general point being that this underprivileged deity would be in much better shape when he had caught up with the spacious soul of the lecturer, who would perforce pray, one supposes, not to his god but for him. All this was set forth with passion, inspired language, and every talent but humor and logic. But, in that very lecture hall, any equally sympathetic and similarly felt exposition of God, freedom, and personal immortality, or of the whole gospel of Jesus Christ, would have been a crime against academic decorum and reckoned by many as worthy only of contempt.

There can be bad practice both ways, of course. Religion itself and the friends of religion can break all the rules of liberal procedure, with methods that violate the whole spirit of liberal education. But the study of religion, in the hands of competent, fair-minded men, can be as wholly committed to the open-minded pursuit of truth and as well observe the rules of argument and scholarly method as any other academic subject can.

What is needed, to see this and to obtain it, is a clear understanding of one essential point about the nature of Christian commitment. The committed Christian surrenders a certain freedom of action. But he does not lose his freedom of inquiry. The allegiance he gives is to One in whose service there is ' perfect freedom.' This includes the right to reason, to investigation, to critical judgments. The Christian can hold with Socrates that the unexamined life is not worth living. But he insists that the examination be complete — that man be studied in a perspective that includes his highest aspirations and insights. Such a field does invite warm differences of opinion. But 'the more controversial a subject and the greater man's inclination to decide and act emotionally without knowledge and reflection, the greater the need for factual instruction and for discipline in objective appraisal.' [17]

'Integration' of learning, moreover, becomes a chief aim in any liberal education concerned with such perspective and wide examination. Wherever thoughtful teachers meet to discuss their common problems, this is likely to be high on the agenda. One of the prime marks of any good education is its fostering our instinct for relating what we know. Universities and colleges have an obligation to be something other than what the late Archbishop of Canterbury, speaking at Oxford, declared them to be — places 'where a multitude of studies are conducted, with no relationship between them except those of simultaneity and juxtaposition.' [18] Many teachers are now inviting both themselves and their studies to a new effort at crossing departmental boundaries, at working in co-operation and considering the unities that do exist among the diversities of knowledge. They are experimenting with many academic devices toward this end.

Religion has real importance as a means to such integration. When it becomes an actual faith, of course, it is a powerful agent in gathering together the varied strands of life and giving both to the world and to the individual a center and direction. But, quite apart from what it confers when it is a way of living, religion has great integrating value when it becomes a phase of liberal study. All life is its concern. It moves through all experience, touching every area of art and industry, both the community and the individual. Dealing with the ordering of goods and looking to responsible relationships, it is involved with all aspects of what Henry More once called 'the rise and fall of life' in the spirit of man.

In this integrating work the Bible has its own rich place. It is not just the key to the whole wealth of allusion in great secular books that have drawn on it over the years. It is itself a compendium of life. It is a forward step in any student's education — and many reared in Christian homes and churches still, unfortunately, have this discovery to make — when he begins to see the Scriptures, not as an austere and solemn book limited to a sphere of its own, but as a treasury of all living interests and varieties. 'If everything else in our language should perish,' Macaulay rightly saw, it would 'alone suffice to show the whole extent of its beauty and power.' The world is in its heart. And something of the same can be said of some of the great sacred books of other religions and of the wide literature of religious themes and interpretation. This is why the rich treasures of the Catholic Church and the Patristic Fathers will continue, despite all differing views, to have a powerful hold on the interest and imagination of men. They have in them almost inexhaustible contact with life, 'the pell-mell of the men and women of Shakespeare's plays,'[19] as well as much that transcends mere variety. 'Stoicism was an education of self-control and of the reason; Neo-Platonism an education of the intuition; but Christianity an education of life as a whole.'[20] Christianity is an integrating experience and draws together our consideration, in terms of what shall or shall not be, of the ordering of our individual and our common world.

All this is the more important now in academic matters, for philosophy has somewhat curtailed its own high effort as a synthesizing agent in liberal education, particularly when its leading thesis is that of logical positivism. For better or worse — according to the teacher and the material he presents — history, literature, and other subjects have been gradually taking over much of the integrating function that philosophy once had. Philosophers themselves are aware of this and they are trying to recover their lost ground. Even so, the inevitable abstractions with which they do and should deal will escape many good men, who must perforce seek integration elsewhere.

Naturalists, in particular, should welcome the integrating efforts of religion — on empirical grounds, if on no other. For religion inquires into the whole range of our nature and experience, the stuff that naturalism seeks to examine. It gives to naturalism some of its most startling data — that one of man's most natural desires, for example, is to be unnatural, to rise beyond the dictates of his old self to some higher self not fully given to him in experience. 'The dignity of man,' said Reinhold Niebuhr in a recent lecture, 'is his freedom, his capacity to make and remake history, to search out all things and to inquire after the meaning of existence. This dignity can be understood only in a dimension deeper and higher than what is known as "nature." Man is not just a slightly more clever animal. He is unique not only in the degree of his practical intelligence or in his inventive genius. His real uniqueness consists in the fact that he can make himself and the world the object of his thought and inquire into the relation of his self to the world.'[21] Man is, in short, the integrating creature. His proper education does not omit a study of his most persistent effort to find his highest meaning.

Amid all the talk of integration, educators are again seeing that our best common response is the response we make to excellence. This is perhaps why Mr. Whitehead's famous statement that education should afford 'the habitual vision of greatness' has caught hold of so many minds. Above all the scattered phenomena, drawing together and to itself the fragments of our nature as the moon draws the sea, excellence shines with its own intrinsic unity. In homely ways and with enduring practical effect, it can be the chief gift a college or a university can give its students — a quality of life, rich in all the images of wonder that learning has to give, conferring standards, creating the right kind of discontent, sealing attachment to good causes, and showing how we can endure, for the sake of some high end, the range of hardship and, what is more pertinent to most of us, the benumbing patter of our trivial chores. This is the great practical work, finally, of all education — to put excellence in men until it can become the *integrity* of their lives.

And we are so made that we see excellence best and understand it most fully when it comes to us in the form of a great person. Our best academy is the noble living and the noble dead. For to most men values become real when they are expressed in somebody's life. One of the best of American educators, Henry Churchill King, of Oberlin, used to recall Kaftan's lectures that defined man's chief problem as the appreciative understanding of the great personalities of history. The highest culture, therefore, 'would be the culture that should enable a man to enter with appreciation and conviction into the deepest and most significant personal life of history.' [22]

To find such a life men have often turned to Greece. Many years ago in a grove near Athens, an olive garden just beyond the city walls, Plato founded his famed Academy. He was in middle life at the time, and Socrates, his master, had been dead a dozen years. But over the Academy brooded the spirit of Socrates, 'the schoolmaster of

Athens who became thereby the schoolmaster of the
Western world.' Much of our minds is the mind he found
men had — mind capable of inductive reason and capable
of forming and realizing concepts that no one before him
had ever expressed. Indeed, the very notion that we might
form concepts at all was, in a striking way, his discovery.
Concerned about action as well as thought, he was a very
practical philosopher. He had a care for civic duties and
the problems of Athenian democracy. He tried to show
young men that the good life was not one of action only
or of thought only — but a harmony of the two, a life of
reflective commitment. He indicated how we might think
of confused appearances and complicated human relationships in universal terms. And his teachings are the ground
of any universal order we may yet achieve.

Socrates was a strange combination. This logical thinker,
with his native skepticism, his keen irony, his zest for ex-
posing fallacies, his astringent Attic salt, had in him a mys-
tical side as well. At the high moments of his own thought
he felt a presence that disturbed him, the surprise of a
power not himself — a kind of ulterior light *within* his
breast. He tried at times to give testimony to this, and
spoke — somewhat unfortunately for our modern ambig-
uous term — of his 'daemon.' He found this surprising
light in others too. It was one of his marks as a great
teacher. He is made to say, in the *Phaedrus,* concerning
the young Lysias: ' My impression of him is that he will
marvelously improve as he grows older, for there is a divine inspiration which will lead him to things higher still.'
He is speaking under a plane tree by the bank of a river.
And he prays before he departs: ' Beloved Pan, and all ye
gods who haunt this place, give me beauty in the inward
soul; and may the outward and the inward man be at one.'

This is the one whose spirit blessed that first academy. Ever since, when men have wished to know the true life of reason and the higher excellence that stands on the top of reason, the surprising inner check and inspiration, they have hoped to share some small portion of the soul of Socrates.

But in another country, still farther to the East, and yet at the center of the known world, there was — to those who have followed Him — a greater than Socrates. By other walks and other olive trees, He too spoke of the fine surprises of the soul. Not of some light that now and then broke in upon Him in fitful gusts of illumination — He made a much more striking claim. Quietly, with a sweet reasonableness that partook of nothing of the madman, doing like Socrates the practical works of virtue, He said: ' I am the light of the world.' ' My Father worketh hitherto, and I work.' Here was the astounding surprise — not just a good man, not just an ethical teacher, but the Son of God, for whom all time was declared to have been preparing. The prophets had foretold that beautiful would be the feet of the messengers. But even when He came, the surprise was not over. And the new surprise was not His death and resurrection; to His followers, immortality seemed the natural logic of a life like His. There was no mystery in that. The surprise lay elsewhere — in that He was not what men expected, a worldly Messiah ready to let Israel go trampling across the nations. Indeed, as has long been noticed, one of the amazing miracles of the New Testament is the fact that the record of Jesus was given to us by men who must at first have been profoundly disappointed in Him. Men who wished to report Him otherwise have given the account of Him that, far beyond their wildest dream, has changed man's life since that time. In spite of themselves and the material things they may at first have wanted, they have left us the re-creative words: 'Whosoever will save his life shall lose it: and whosoever will lose his life for my sake shall find it.' 'The kingdom of heaven is like to a grain of mustard seed, which a man took, and sowed in his field: which indeed is the least of all seeds: but when it is grown, it is the greatest among herbs, and becometh a tree, so that the birds of the air come and lodge in the branches thereof.' 'The kingdom of God cometh not with observation: Neither shall they say, Lo here! or, lo there! for, behold, the kingdom of God is within you.'

To those who believe in Jesus Christ these are the great words of integration. They have earned the right, out of a tremendous history, to be examined among the excellent things offered in any liberal education. Already they have proved universal enough to be part of the inquiry of a university. To omit them is to forfeit any claim to be a university at all.

What, then, can the friends of religion or those who, friendly or not, see its fair claim on liberal education ask by way of a practical program? What can they expect of universities and private colleges not affiliated with a Church? They should first realize, of course, that a considerable amount has already been done. Reports on these programs are available from several universities and colleges,[23] and our concern here is not with detail but with principles.

Some Christians believe that the only answer lies in frankly Christian universities, not necessarily or even advisedly returning to the synthesis of the Middle Ages or depreciating experimental quest for new knowledge, but wholly Christian in character and aim. A clear case can, of course, be made for such universities, and no Christian should despair of having them. But for the institutions we now have this is not in the immediate future a likely program, for one plain reason: we do not yet have the really Christian society that gives common sanction to such universities. Moreover, universities have become such tremendous places, doing such a wide variety of professional and vocational work, that they are not, in their total working, quickly susceptible to any deeply felt ideal except — and that no mean one — the ideal of work well done. Universities in America, especially those receiving public funds, are pretty sure to be something other than what a devoted Christian might like them to be.

And even were it possible to turn our universities overnight into officially Christian bodies, resuming more of their early character, their acquired unity would at present be a fictitious unity at best. Dr. John Baillie has pointed out the dishonesty and the danger of any premature attempt ' to impose upon our common life the outward semblance of a unity which it does not inwardly possess.' [24] And another British critic gives similar warning:

The modern university is becoming more and more conscious of its disunity and confusion and may be tempted to seek for itself a spurious unity which is imposed upon the life of the institution from above. In this country this would still probably take the form of a ' Christian ' ideology, but one which had been accommodated to the prejudices or doubts of half-believers, humanists, and rationalists. It would probably be linked vaguely with abstractions like truth, beauty, and goodness, and with ' democratic ' ideals and national aspirations. It would probably make a virtue of indefiniteness in order to secure the maximum of agreement and would

serve as a cloak to cover up all the real differences between men which the university should exist to bring
into the light of honest discussion and critical examination. The Christian should give no encouragement to
any move in this direction, as he may be tempted to do
under the illusion that it would serve his witness to the
Gospel in the university by so doing. Until the present
spiritual confusion shows some sign of being genuinely
resolved, the Christian will be more concerned to em-
phasize the importance of the real freedom of the university than its need for unity.[25]

It is on this real freedom of the university that religion
has its claim. It can properly demand — and do it now —
that the university exhibit the religious aspect of life and
stop ignoring it. Without yielding any of its freedom to ecclesiastical authority or in any way impairing itself, the
university can give a hearing to the faith whose aims it so
often shares in its desire to foster the ' good ' in man and
in society. There is nothing gained by clouding the issue.
Liberal rationalism, humanism, scientism, and Christianity are not the same thing. On any campus the men who
hold one or another of these rival views get on well enough
together; they share common tasks, they have humor and
tolerance in ample measure, for the most part, and they
are bound together by many similar ideals. But they stand,
in the long run, for very different things and very different views of life. They should not, for their own intellectual health, all pretend to look the same, however benevolent and congenial the play of their common humanity or
' simple gregariousness.' They should be permitted to compete and to compare and to learn important truths from
one another, and they should give their students the civ-

ilizing privilege of watching them do so and of doing so
in turn. But if the dominating tone of a university is that
of an exclusive secularism, whatever its particular forms,
the chance of any real hearing for religion is almost nil.
Any university has men of all parties and philosophies.
Yet, as far as the curriculum goes, the Christian contingent either often accepts, or is often reduced to, an ob-
scurity and silence that make students feel it has no more
meaning or importance than it seems to have. Such im-
balance is not liberal, nor any credit to free universities.

The place of religion in the curriculum is crucial. To say
this is not to discredit the work of college chaplains, the
various campus foundations set up by the Churches, or
extracurricular projects of any kind. The Churches should
encourage these voluntary agencies more than they have.
Specialized and technical education particularly needs a
sense of ends and aims; it can learn much from the Christian doctrine of vocation for responsible human life. Yet,
as President Nason says, the trouble with extracurricular
efforts is they do not go far enough:

They cannot go far enough, and the belief that their
existence discharges the responsibility of the institution
for religion is a major source of weakness. Students who
come to college with strong religious convictions will
take an active part in one or more of these undergraduate activities. The majority, however, will unconsciously
look to see what the authorities judge to be important.
If religion is relegated to the role of a not-too-important
sideshow, if its part in our intellectual and emotional
tradition is ignored, and if the members of the faculty
act with indifference, whether deliberate or uncon-
scious, toward those questions of ultimate import which

no discipline can escape and on which religion has had much to say, then it is small wonder that a majority of students will go their way, troubled perhaps and a little uneasy in the absence of answers, upon the assumption that religion does not matter.[26]

An adequate place in the curriculum means a department of religion, with personnel of high quality, comparable to that of other academic departments. It means a sufficient offering of courses, not all necessarily within the department — in the Bible, comparative religion, the philosophy and psychology of religion, Christian ethics, Church history (of the greatest use to students in a half dozen other departments), the history of Christian thought, and the like. The course in Bible, incidentally, would be more than a course in ' the Bible as literature ' — too often, as Mr. Eliot has observed, the mere admiration of ' a monument over the grave of Christianity.' It would be a course in the Hebrew-Christian conception of life.

Genuine curricular acceptance of religion would involve also the securing of some adequate attention to religion in the other courses of the university where it is germane. There are many such courses, where consideration of religion, necessary to the understanding of the matter at hand, is not something for the teacher to include or ignore according to his own whim, but to take account of because it is his professional duty. And in the new ' core ' courses and divisional courses designed primarily for a student's ' general ' education, the place of religion is clear.

Courses in religion, in the hands of competent men, can be taught without violating the spirit of free inquiry. Teaching need not be preaching here any more than in economics, politics, and other subjects on which we feel deeply. Frankness and sympathy for a subject need not mean narrowness and pietism. The true scholar — who, after all, is the determining factor — will feel in religion as in other fields, his appropriate obligations. In this connection, the writer can pay his own personal tribute to what he saw at first hand, the development at Princeton University of a department of Religion, under the direction of Professor George F. Thomas, which has shown how religious knowledge can be presented, sympathetically and without dilution, with fairness to many points of view, with academic propriety, and with an enrichment of other undergraduate studies.

Here, as throughout the university, the problem of securing free play of the mind, is a problem of the teacher's own culture. It is a problem that works both ways. And it centers in the graduate school that prepares the teacher — though it is fair to admit that no graduate school can be expected to repair in three or four years the ravages of a bad education received in the sixteen years preceding it. But there can be little hope for any integration of knowledge wide enough to include religion within the working domain of other subjects until more teachers, in addition to their specialty, have something else also. This is a well-known problem, where all of us have sinned to some degree, and the answer is not a facile one. What we can hope for is at least a greater breadth of sympathy — the prelude to any added breadth of culture. Our present university scene is not without hope on this score. The graduate schools are re-examining their responsibility to help to produce teachers who are more than specialists. We can at least, as this general defect in the preparation of teachers touches religion, ask an end to the particular kind of secularism that, as Chancellor Hutchins points out, 'besets the higher learning in America,' the notion that religion is insignificant, outmoded, and equivalent to superstition. ' This kind of secularism higher education can and should repel. If a college or university is going to think about important things, then it must think about religion. It is perhaps not necessary that all the faculty should be religious; it is necessary that most of them, at least, should take religion seriously.' [27]

Certainly religion itself need not suffer if examined in a university curriculum. It is often argued that

morality and religion are so personal to each individual, so fragile and elusive, that their essence must be lost when they are subjected to historical and critical analysis. The same argument is sometimes used against critical and historical study of the arts; artistic quality also is declared to be so fragile that it cannot survive careful investigation. This sentimental notion is indefensible. All thoughtful students of the arts acknowledge the benefit they have received from their study. There is abundant evidence to support a similar conclusion concerning the study of morality and religion. Distinctive qualities can, of course, be apprehended only through direct acquaintance. To divorce the study of morality and religion from actual moral conduct and religious worship, or to believe that an understanding of what morality and religion really involve can be achieved by mere external observation, without sympathetic insight, would be foolish and uninformed. A liberal study, however, involves no such divorce or belief. Liberal schools and colleges can and should provide moral and religious instruction which will enable students to escape from slavish conventions or complete ignorance, by putting at their disposal relevant facts and by teaching them to interpret these facts in a rational and informed manner.[28]

Nor, finally, is a course in religion made impossible by the variety of belief or unbelief represented by the students in even a single university classroom. Actually, as Dr. Bernard Iddings Bell once found when he was teaching in a university, most of the students really had no religion that involved much thinking, 'no religion about which one could talk intelligently. With rare exceptions, all they possessed in the way of religion was some vague loyalty to an ecclesiastical group — about half of them had this; a number of prejudices, chiefly against communions other than that with which they were vaguely affiliated.' With the permission of the faculty, Dr. Bell tried to teach these students 'a little about what religion has always been and still is and about what religious people of the major faiths today believe and do and why they believe and do it.' He stressed Judaism and Christianity as the religions of the West. 'As the course went on the result was usually that each student understood more fully the implications of his own inchoate religion and also came to a fair appreciation of the practices and beliefs of those brought up in ways different from his own. It deepened conviction and cultivated tolerance.' [29]

Here is the hint of how universities can assist the Churches in what is their most conspicuous twentieth-century effort — the new ecumenical movement. There is nothing more hopeful on our contemporary scene than the earnest desire to bring a spirit of unity and common purpose among the different denominations. Whatever else it does, the academic study of religion can help here. For such study will not be found by dwelling on denominational peculiarities. It will thereby miss some interesting and valuable things. But it will more than compensate by centering its attention on the main values and large beliefs of religion and the Church rather than on the minutiae of the Churches. And this appraisal from outside itself can do religion great good and show the Churches what they hold in common and the common work they yet have to do. For religion, like men, sometimes has to be reminded of its own best self.

Who can bring about the real place of religion in the universities and the secular colleges? Trustees, administrators, faculty, alumni, and students who care. At one university it was a faculty committee of interested men, appointed by a sympathetic administrator; they reported to the faculty a plan for establishing courses in religion. Elsewhere the impulse has come from the administration or the alumni. Whatever the group, it may include both believers and nonbelievers. The latter may have no concern about religion itself; but they have, as scholars and lovers of truth — as do the men of faith, one hopes — a care for what is adequate and what is fair in liberal education.

CHAPTER

4

LIBERAL EDUCATION AND RELIGION:
THE CHURCH COLLEGE

WHATEVER ELSE IT DOES, the Church college should know what it is. Or, more modestly, it should know what it ought to be. That very clarity is at least a kind of oasis to anyone following the vexed matters of this book. It is a clarity that, for the Church colleges themselves, raises both opportunity and difficulty. It can be the source of greatness and littleness, of imagination or the lack of it. But for the historian and the student of higher education it is not unpleasant to find, alongside the almost inevitable confusions and complexities of secular education, a kind of higher learning that has its central faith and therefore a fairly plain chart of what it is supposed to do. Even those who cannot share its faith and purpose must be grateful for something unmistakable enough to be clearly disavowed.

The historian, of course, finds another claim on his attention — one this book will not detail: the extraordinary part the Church colleges have had in the story of our country. The *Cambridge Modern History* may choose to ignore entirely the missionary movement which for two hundred years has influenced civilization and international life.[1] But no competent historian can dare pass over the

Church college in America. It is interesting, for example, to read the amusing yet fair account two of our best historians give to even the small colleges, mostly projects of the Church, that arose and flourished — though only a fifth of them have survived — in the Eastern and Midwestern states, both North and South, before the War Between the States:

It was the heyday of the small, rural college with six to a dozen professors and one to three hundred students; of six o'clock chapel, prescribed classical-mathematical course, with chemistry and physics the most popular subjects next to Greek, and a smattering of French and German; 'philosophical apparatus,' mineralogical cabinet and collection of stuffed birds; Freshman metaphysics, Saturday recitations on Paley's *Evidences of Christianity* followed by dismal Puritan Sabbath, relieved by periodical religious revivals and tremendous drinking bouts; literary and debating societies encouraged, and Greek-letter fraternities discouraged by the faculty; well selected libraries of ancient and modern classics (Voltaire locked up); botanizing and fossil-hunting excursions over the countryside, ingenious hazing and amusing pranks, but no organized sports. . . . The average statesman and professional man of the Northern states completed his formal education at a small college, whose curriculum in many instances was not equal to that of a first-class secondary school today. Foreign visitors compared these institutions with Oxford, Cambridge, or Göttingen, and laughed or sneered. But for an integrated education, one that cultivates manliness or makes gentlemen as well as scholars, one that disciplines the social affections and trains young men to faith in God, consideration for his fellow man, and respect for learning, America has never had the equal of her little hill-top colleges.[2]

In this early day, and certainly in their later and very different form, the Church colleges, out of all proportion to their size or to their worldly goods, have educated men and women for places of leadership here and over the world in every walk of life. It is a familiar story, and America has nothing more exclusively American.

Of the colleges and universities now open in the United States, 40.16 per cent of the total have direct relation to the Churches, with varying degrees of Church control; 26.97 per cent are privately endowed, many of these having once been established by Churches from which they have broken away but with which they often retain sentimental ties or active sympathy; and 32.87 per cent are supported by public funds and are state or municipally controlled. About 49.4 per cent of our students are enrolled in public universities and colleges.

Church-related colleges are, to be sure, not all alike. They vary greatly in size, though practically all may still be classed as 'small.' They reflect many differences of form and substance, of endowment and plant, of educational aim. Being human, they all know they have not at many times fulfilled either their religious or their academic purpose. They fall short, in one way or another, of the good thing we intend to say of them in this chapter. Yet, for all their differences and their shortcomings, they have strong areas of general agreement, and a central view of life that gives them a more than superficial unity. Most of them would recognize, we feel, the outline we are now to consider of their purpose, their successes, and their

102 THE MIND'S ADVENTURE

problems. For they have many things in common.

A Church college begins with a commitment to a divine truth which those who found or perpetuate it believe has been revealed to men and has been tested by both thought and experience. It is a truth become real and valid for them; and to proceed with life on any other basis would be pretentious and insincere. There is still much they do not understand — mysteries unsolved and much yet to be discovered. Their own religion is a source not yet exhausted. They are barred from no scrutiny, however severe, of this faith itself. They believe, even so, that we already know something that gives meaning and center to our span of life — that there has been a great event in history; that truth, as we know it and search it out, is ' in order to goodness' and to a reality that is behind all the manifestations of our lives. They believe, in short, that life is sacred in a world wherein God has given them freedom to decide for themselves if all this be so.

The Church college holds, essentially, that behind all life is a Creator, whose creation we and the world are. He has revealed Himself as a God of justice in a moral universe that makes man a responsible being, but also as a God of love, in Jesus Christ, His Son. In this stunning miracle of love, imperfect man, the mark of sin upon him, finds, beyond his own free choice of good and evil, the instrument of his true redemption and a compelling invitation to the renewal of himself and to immortal life. And there is a creative partnership with God possible for man in history, a share in practical goodness and a creative purpose.

The Christian college will be, therefore, a community existing around a group of learners, both teachers and students, who confess Jesus Christ as their Saviour and Lord. They are engaged in a serious search for the knowledge of God and His universe and His demands upon human life. Though they control their environment for this specific purpose, they are not exclusive or self-contained. They invite to their inquiry those who may not hold their premises or yet share their practical commitment. They will give others time to test, accept, or reject what they believe, and put no halter or blinder upon minds alien to their own. They will not hurry strangers to their faith to throw about the great words that they themselves only imperfectly comprehend — the deepening convictions of their own hearts and minds. They will not try to cheat intellectually either the stranger or themselves or set traps such as the eighteenth-century poet James Beattie set for his little son when he planted cress in the garden so that it would come up to spell the child's name and thus persuade him by the argument from design. But those who do not share the community faith must not, in turn, resent it if the Christian community of the college has some decent care and friendly desire to share with them what it believes is an authentic view of human life.

A Church college, augmenting its belief, will have its valuable and necessary agencies. It will have its chapel and church as an opportunity for worship, its instruction in religion, its environment that tries to reflect Christian principles. Religion is strikingly a problem of paying attention to what one seeks or knows; practical devotions, both public and private, are essential to its growth. But, even so, Christian education is not just education plus a set of rules, prescribed courses in the Bible, and opportunities for worship. 'Unfortunately,' writes Dr. Frank H. Caldwell, ' this is perhaps the most widely prevalent conception of Christian education, even among church people, and often among ministers. . . . If this idea of Chris-

tian education is to be considered as valid, then the cost
of administration and of instruction in the fields of mathematics, physics, chemistry, history, English, and all the
other subjects outside the field of Bible and religion, is too
great a price to pay just for the privilege of having required courses in Bible and compulsory chapel attendance. The concept of addition can be devastating when
applied to Christianity. For Christianity is no little " plus "
added on to secular life and thought. It is no thin icing
spread over the outside of a black cake to make it look
white. Christianity is basic. It is normative. It has to do
with the essence of life and with the whole of life. To
compartmentalize it is to imprison it, and to nullify it.' ³

If there be a God, the truth of all the world is His truth,
and religion is not a fragment or phase of the educational
process, but its permeating factor and its inner unity.
Christian education is thus a study of all life for the discovery of divine truth. In terms of the investigation carried on, the methods used, there is, of course, no such
thing as 'Christian chemistry' or 'Christian biology.'
There are ideas and data in the social studies, history,
literature, and philosophy that no one can ignore. Both
the secular and the Christian scholar will deal with the
same facts in his field; but the facts, once determined, will
then begin to mean vastly different things to the *men*
looking at them. It cannot be otherwise; for, given his
major premise — which he is always free to examine in the
light of all available knowledge — the Christian cannot
pretend that God's creation is other or less than it is. He
will share Newman's view that God has 'relations of His
own towards the subject-matter of each particular science
which the book of knowledge unfolds.' Religious truth is
thus ' not only a portion, but a condition of general knowl-

edge.' To blot it out is to unravel the web of education. ' It
is, according to the Greek proverb, to take the spring from
out of the year.' ⁴ For these reasons, the true Church college, as Professor Clarke, of Daillam, has been keen to
point out, does not ' *have* a religious program. It *is* a religious program.'

Simultaneously, a Church college is also an educational
program. It has an obligation to liberal learning and to
free inquiry. The Church college I know best was dedi-
cated, for example, in 1866, in its articles of incorporation,
to ' the promotion of sound learning and education under
religious influences,' and was conceived of ' as an institution with broad foundations and facilities equal to the
best in the land, capable of preparing men for every department of life.' That was a large order, and it still is. But
it represents the double task assigned to all Church colleges by founders who cared about both learning and religion. A college fails in its purpose if it discharges one
task and not the other.

As an academic, and often as a religious, community a
small college knows some of its inevitable handicaps. It
should not try to gloss them over. It will, in all likelihood,
lack the cultural variety of the university — lectures, con-
certs, exhibitions, the profusion of eminent names in many
fields. If the college be located away from a city, one of
its real losses will be that of the privilege of browsing
easily in a large bookshop. But a college conscious of
these things can do much to take up the slack and keep
a life from the outside flowing in some measure through
its own community. After all, it will have fewer distrac-
tions from its main task. And many a faculty member,
coming to a small college, has found compensation for the
loss of the stimulation he had in working in a large de-

partment in the more accessible association the smaller place offers him with men in fields other than his own.

Moreover, a Church college usually provides a friendly community of close human exchanges — both students and faculty feeling the warmth of a kind of 'family' life — with the common interests and questions that foster broad perspective among an academic society. Religion has its own remembrance of things past, its link with all the fruitful centuries; it will not easily permit the severance, in any fields of learning, from our cultural heritage or encourage the provincial 'presentism' which is the death of liberal study. By its nature, it looks to ideas and leading principles, and is the enemy of scattered information that comes to no head or relationship. It is relatively free from the necessity of doing anything on so large and expensive a scale that it must be bound for a long time by what it has done wrong. By its own simplicity and flexibility it can, as more than one college observer has noticed, get out of its own ruts fairly easily. By the same token, it is free, within budgetary limits, to experiment and do creative pioneering of its own in both the content and the method of liberal studies. These are no small blessings.

Two problems, however, are crucial for the Church college that wants to do its educational work well. The first of these is its faculty. The faith and hope of any college rest ultimately in the men and women who teach there. It lives or dies by its appointments, and in no place is the task of appointing teachers harder than in a Church-related college.

For a good Church college makes a high demand of anyone who teaches there. First of all, he must be either a Christian himself or a person who is at least sympathetic with religious inquiry and the main ethical principles

Christianity holds. Not just anybody will do. Men who, only because of their technical proficiency in some field of scholarship, would be welcome and comfortable in the complexity of a university would not serve a Church college well or be happy in doing so. The Church college seeks, or should seek, men with balanced interest in scholarship and teaching — and with something more. They must, of course, be authentic professionally, living off the fresh life of new fact and the imaginative synthesis of the facts they already know. As scholars, they should represent the critical spirit, the dispassionate mind, and the reflection that should precede and accompany commitment. But, in addition to their respect and care for knowledge, they must be men who know that beyond the world of information there lies a world of value and deep loyalties — that men were born to hate some things and to love others; that there are causes and affections to which men of good will may conceivably be bound forever. And it helps if they really care about young people.

One frequently hears scornful talk of men who have held chairs in small colleges without adequate preparation — ministers who have failed in the ministry and found it convenient to teach, men whose chief claims to a professorship were good hearts and native piety rather than intellectual distinction. Carrying on their classes year after year without research or the refurbishing of their old lectures, they were long on sweetness and short on light. But pedantry and mental laziness are not the monopoly of Church colleges; one supposes that pedantry and laziness have been found in secular institutions as well. Almost every college and university has had its dry and dusty days.

But almost every small college has other memories — of men and women who, out of plain devotion, were teachers beyond all just demand of their calling. Many of them preferred the cause they served to more conspicuous places to which they might easily have aspired. Some of them occupied the famous ' sofa ' rather than a ' chair,' and taught more subjects than one mortal should be called upon to teach; but they made no pretension to what they did not know and plainly marked their boundaries. They often, through the sheer variety of the chores laid on them, acquired a liberal knowledge that would have shamed narrower scholars of far greater fame. All they thought and did was illumined with a love of God and men that made them often greater in themselves than anything they did or said. And what they were was contagious.

The writer was fortunate in knowing men who had this kind of consecration to their calling. Some of them were scholars who could easily have held university chairs. They did a prodigious amount of work, both in their own fields and in the general life of the campus community. One was a biologist, one a philosopher, one a chemist, one a classicist, one a professor of literature, and so on; but all were fired as by some common flame. It was not necessary to unlearn anything they taught; to my best knowledge, they obscured no known truth or even a hypothesis pertinent to their field. They gave full statement of views they did not hold themselves. Yet their students caught, both by direction and indirection, the faith that sustained and animated them. And men now scattered all over the world today know whom I am speaking of and will bless their names.

The Church had a duty to such men, and it did not do its duty. It permitted them to work on the merest margin of subsistence, a margin not good for them or for the cause they served. They almost never complained, and they would not have been spoiled or corrupted by enough to let them work reasonably free from worry, to be able to travel more than they did, buy the books they needed so that they could mark them for their own, and enjoy a few of the amenities of life. Even now, in our supposedly more worldly time, the Church college still has its consecrated men, whose first thought is not of what they earn but of what they do. But for the sake of any education worthy to be set forth in God's name, the Church must do more to enable the teachers in its colleges to come to their own best. Unless this cardinal point is met, our Church colleges by and large cannot hope to compete with secular and public institutions or be 'equal to the best in the land.' A miracle of sacrifice cannot go on being a miracle forever. And, if it can, it should not be allowed to do so. In every Church college there are men whose best has not been brought out of them because no proper investment has been made in them.

Specifically, the teachers in our Church colleges must have greater opportunity for research and sabbatical leaves. Men who would prefer to serve the Church in its schools and colleges feel they cannot be divorced from university centers without too great sacrifice of their professional integrity. But, with some generous provision for research leaves given to those who could establish their claim to them, the Church college can give to a certain number of professors so inclined the privilege of carrying on firsthand investigation. Its faculty will always be a varied faculty, and there should be no false pressure on a teacher to engage in insincere puttering merely to increase a trivial bibliography or become great by 'pagination.' The lust for publication is not the same thing as the

lust for learning. Nevertheless, a college will be the richer
for at least some teachers who can do first-class research.
They should not all be in the universities. In some ways
the small college needs their leaven more than a university does. They inspire students by example; and they
give the college a membership in the larger world of
scholars, of which it should wish to be a part. And even
for those who do not publish the results of their inquiry,
time off from teaching is needed to restore them. No un-
renewed reservoir, however large, 'can long feed living
water to running brooks.' No teacher, however clever, can
live successfully off mere 'inspiration' and a yellow stock
of old knowledge.

Closely related and almost one with the problem of its
faculty is the second academic concern of the Church college — the keeping alive of a spirit of free inquiry. We
have already discussed the Christian's freedom of open
examination, even of his own faith, in considering the
compatibility of religion and liberal education generally.
This same freedom is imperative in a Church college.
Above all else, the college must not be a citadel of the
closed mind. It must welcome the exposure of its students
to all scholarly opinion and to any important idea under
consideration by mankind. Neat selection and indoctrina-
tion will not do; nor will obscurantism of any kind. A
Church college can have warmth in its teaching and be
entirely unashamed of the high emotion that belongs to
high truth. Its department of religion need not, for example, out of some strained intellectuality, acquire the
genius a certain British critic was reputed to have — the
knack of presenting Christianity so that it was recogniz-
able neither to its friends nor to its foes. But this does not
mean the 'namby-pamby sentimentalism and a very un-

attractive " muscularity " ' [5] that often pass for Christian experience.

Too often, one fears, students are sent to Church colleges on the happy assumption that the college will conspire in an amiable plot against the student's mind — that it will pass over or tidy up the unpleasant aspects of a subject or the ugly facts human beings must face at some time or other. Certainly some of these surprises should not be left for later life, when they come with a rude jolt to any 'protected' philosophy or to a mind barred from its own experience. This does not mean injecting into a college course all the rotten stuff published for rottenness' sake or professors smacking their lips like overgrown adolescents over something they think shocking. But it does mean ducking away from no truth that embarrasses one's favorite intellectual conclusion. Someone remarked once that if expurgation ran away with itself, we should soon have a vest-pocket Steinbeck called 'The Seedless Grapes of Wrath.' But little good would be served if the 'seedless grapes' of learning were the staple diet of Church colleges.

The duty of the college to a student does not lie in shielding him from disturbing facts or even alleged facts. Its duty is to help him place all data in some perspective, to help him proceed to the second step of *thinking about* the known facts in the light of all the rest we know — including the best we know — as men. Actually, the main shock any inquiring college student is likely to receive is the shock of new knowledge which seems, at first, to invalidate his own personality. The function of education is, among other things, to help keep alive during this difficult period his own reality as a person; to remind him that persons are the only judge the facts have and confer on them their only meaning; to see to it that he somehow is not absent from the symbols of great human value and those things that light up the human spirit and do it honor. Many of these things will be, of course, the substance of his liberal studies and the part religion has in them.

A Church college knows no blind alleys down which it need fear to look. The Christian, as part of his faith, believes that 'God has spoken his truth to men' and that this truth has made him free. His faith should therefore risk all competition. It should scorn to be as timid and nervous as that of the Southern church which asked all its members to spend at least two hours reading the Bible for every one hour they listened to a liberal lecturer — the lecturer in turn being quite surprised that anyone should reckon his words twice as powerful as Holy Writ. A Church college need not stand on 'made' ground. It can welcome all the evidence. It should insist only that all the evidence really be there, including man's deepest insight and his highest aspirations.

A Church college is also a community. In such a community much of its vital education will occur. Dean Gilkey, commenting on the various efforts at reconciling the truth of science with the truth of religion, begins to wonder if Whitehead 'is not deeply right in his brief but profound chapter on this matter: whether the most valuable and enduring reconciliations are not those worked out functionally rather than theoretically, in the realm of personality and social experience where so many diverse attitudes and approaches to reality prove to be both compatible and supplementary, by individuals and groups and generations who try to learn both to think scientifically and to live religiously.' [6] The failure of Saint Simeon

Stylites on his desert pillar was his missing, among other things, what he could have learned from other people.

The work a college does, at any rate, is not confined to the classroom. It is done within the whole experience of the community — in common worship, in practical projects undertaken, in community service, and in the whole variety of extracurricular life. In one sense, Christianity cannot be studied at all; it must be lived, however imperfect that effort be. And one learns out of association with those who are making such an effort something that cannot be learned from books alone. 'If any man will do his will, he shall know of the doctrine, whether it be of God' is a great Christian text, implying the laboratory work inevitable in real Christian education. As Dr. H. H. Horne, out of his wide learning and wide experience, used to say, 'The best argument for Christianity is a Christian.' [7]

The Christian community of the Church college will include every member — professors, cooks, deans, students, janitors, presidents, trustees, and groundmen. It should include, if possible, one first-rate night watchman who has powers as a friendly philosopher as well as a policeman. Head residents in dormitories are teachers in their own right, and best by example. One of the valuable members of our own campus community was an Italian bricklayer who for thirty-five years was a living demonstration of joy in one's work. He was employed by the college in 1911, after temporary service to a construction company as watchman on a campus building project. He was under strict orders to let no one pass, and in the light of this commission he refused one evening to admit the president of the college and some guests. The president was so impressed by this fidelity, even though it seemed a little overdone, that he promptly gave Angelo Santoro a full-time job. Over the years, doing all kinds of work as if it were some high privilege, the light shining from something within himself in delightful and moving ways, this Roman Catholic workman taught the campus community, the majority of whom were Presbyterians, a lot that both John Calvin and John Knox never quite made clear. His remarkable portrait now hangs beside the pictures of the men and women the college is glad to honor — as it should. He was one of our best 'professors.'

Naturally, a Church college will have certain standards for its own community and will not try to be all things to all men. Therefore, its life is not likely to be at all points the life of what a sophomore thinks of as the 'world.' The sophomore has, of course, one consolation — that, more than he may guess or the college authorities may always know, the 'world' may reach him, for it has great enterprise and a knack of penetrating even the campus of a Church college. In 1950, the world is generally pretty much with us, or at least next door. Standing for Christian ethics, trying to convey the power of great creative renunciations, the Church college has some things to make very plain. But, while maintaining its own character, it is fortunate if it can also keep its humor, its understanding, and, along with necessary firmness, an almost infinite patience. It will do well to recall one of Thornton Wilder's wisest observations: 'Of all forms of genius, goodness has the longest awkward age;' [8] or perhaps even Emerson's reminder, which Dean Wicks of Princeton, who knew many an undergraduate's problems, always liked: 'You should never try to make another person like yourself, because you know and I know and God knows that one like you is enough.'

A Church college will give opportunity for worship. It will imply that prayer has many grounds of validity — among others, the fact that Christ, who was expert in spiritual matters and whose insight went deeper than anyone else's a Christian knows, prayed; and therefore, as it has been suggested, one who would learn what He knew may well follow His example. It will afford students the chance to hear the best Church music and to realize that good taste, which may include simplicity, is a good point in any honoring of God. It will suggest the idea of 'the fellowship of the Church' — not always an easy or welcome idea at nineteen. There are moments in undergraduate life, not always dropped at graduation, when a sudden rush of intellect makes the church, a homely sermon, the singing of hymns, and the like, seem a very provincial and unsophisticated experience in comparison with ventures into art, music, literature, and philosophy, the voyaging of one's mind into 'strange seas of thought alone.' This is a not wholly deplorable elevation of the wits, however, and when culture stops panting and becomes something genuine in itself, it often perceives both the religious and the personal truth of the Lord's promise of some added presence and insight that do come to men, however homely the circumstances, when two or three are gathered together in His name.

Two tasks any Church college must ask of its students — without which their religious experience will be very thin. The first is their doing a decent amount of honest academic work. Beneath all high talk about the higher learning, one plain fact remains — the first job of even higher education is to get a student before an open book and keep him there, captured by it, for fifteen consecutive minutes. If this can be done by persuasion, by the awakening of interest, all the better; but, whatever the means, it must be done. Not all the legends of undergraduates enjoying merely a four-year housing venture are true, however. The great majority of students in our institutions of higher learning, contrary to the impression given by the movies and by certain educators who have fun calling them names, do justify the expenditure made in their behalf. But there are still far too many going to college out of insincere or trivial reasons — too many willing, for example, to do less than a minimum forty or forty-five hours a week on their studies, including time spent in class or laboratory. It can always be argued, of course, that these wholly delightful participants in 'general culture' get something out of college, something usually described as 'a lot of good.' The trouble is that they get something else too — habits of laziness, flimsiness, and superficiality that seriously hurt them at the core of their own natures. Society in general, let alone the Church, cannot fairly be asked to pay for the spawning of parasites on the social order for four however amiable years. There is a minimum decency of honest work even for the educated. As Woodrow Wilson said long ago, character is still the by-product of work well done.

The other thing a Church college can ask is that its students take a more than ordinary responsibility for a genuine campus democracy with some care for its government. The campus of a Church college has, by its very nature, a care for personality, a respect for opinions of differing members and for human significance. It has a right to expect, therefore, an effort on the part of its members to work out some kind of democratic government for themselves while they are still in college. Whatever they do will be some index of what they will do later in the world. As Oliver Wendell Holmes saw, 'The axis of the earth sticks out visibly through the centre of each and every town or city.' A political science major worrying about Washington or the United Nations, while he condones infantile irresponsibility in campus government, is not a happy exhibit in either secular or Christian education.

Christian education knows also the importance of counseling and the place religion has in helping a student with himself and his own problems. As Professor Outler says, in his admirable pamphlet on this subject, we do not have, in counseling, the painful choice between a Christian account of man and 'the materialistic and mechanistic assumptions of the prevailing systems of psychopathology, psychoanalysis, and psychiatry.' [9] The possible task — and Professor Outler supports his thesis in striking detail — is that of 'assimilating the practical wisdom of the psychologist, however secular and mechanistic his own world-view may be, to the basic and perennial first principles of the Christian faith and Christian theology.' [10] The total counseling program of a Church college — academic orientation, vocational or personal guidance — is, like the college itself, a religious program. This does not mean, of course, that the counselor will be forever talking about religion. He may not refer directly to it at all. But it will be the informing background of everything he does and says. A student will not be left to deal with himself or his work out of a smaller or less meaningful context than the Christian view of life can give. There will be realistic, practical concern for a student's needs and interest; but there will be also a suggestion of some secret other than himself, a hint — and often more than a hint — of that 'selfless self' which is Christianity's richest and most fruitful paradox.

Moreover, the heightening and added enjoyment Christianity can give to life can be given to learning also. Those who can accept the Christian view of the world know the illumination and deepened appreciation that come with it. For Christianity is no constricted, life-denying pietism, some celestial frost that shrivels the bloom of the world. It asks surrender of many selfish things in life, not that we may obey an edict, but that we may be really free for fullness of living and these deeper appreciations.

> It is this which made the fortune of Christianity, — its gladness, not its sorrow; not its assigning the spiritual world to Christ, and the material world to the devil, but its drawing from the spiritual world a source of joy so abundant that it ran over upon the material world and transfigured it.[11]

This is the religion that can light up a liberal education — conferring new powers of appreciation, new zest for research, and fresh knowledge. It brings together what should never have been divorced, the spiritual world and whatever in the material world deserves to endure. It bridges the spirit of the Renaissance and the spirit of the Puritan. It honors intelligence, yet asks of reason its 'most exalted mood.' It enriches, while it does all these things, the homely joy of our daily human associations. And, as religion steps up the meaning of life, it steps up also the meaning of liberal studies.

It also makes education seem possible to those who might otherwise turn from it in discouragement. Many a student, seeing minds more receptive than his own, unhappy at his own limited talent, is tempted to give up all effort. But, if he believes that behind all life there is for us some divine relationship, if a mind and love behind the world have some knowledge to give of universal importance, it will be nonsense to assume that these great communications are reserved only for the few. Techniques and philosophies may be beyond him. He can be a complete and modest realist on that score. But the important concepts and ideas that make a difference in the life of men and in the quality of their spirits — these can be comprehended. There is among all men a wide community of essential understanding. And we are helped too because the great thinkers and writers, sensing these universal truths, slave away at their expression until they make them plain and clear to the men for whom the truth was intended. To the Christian the world is in process of revelation. He knows, in his most discouraged moments, that he dare not quit too soon his own effort at comprehending. The poets and prophets and philosophers have minds and souls that, as Sir Arthur Quiller-Couch once said so well, ' throw out filaments more delicate than ours, vibrating to far messages which they bring home, to report them to us . . . and when they write it, we call their report literature. But it is by the spark in us that we read it; and not all the fire of God that was in Shakespeare can dare to patronize the little spark in me.' [12] This too can be part of the faith of liberal education, in which perception takes many forms and the race is not always to the swift. ' Many prophets and kings have desired to see those things which ye see, and have not seen them; and to hear those things which ye hear, and have not heard them.'

What does the college owe the Church to which it is related? The double effort of trying to become a better place of higher learning, honoring and serving true scholarship, and also of deepening its own unapologetic character as a center of genuine Christianity. The college should seek as its product those of whom the Church can be proud — free and responsible citizens who love both truth and the loyalties to which truth has led them. For 'the educated Christian mind should be the most free even as it is under the greatest debt and possessed of the greatest responsibility.'[13] A fair number of the graduates of a Church college should serve the Church in full-time tasks, at home and overseas. But the college should also contribute an even greater number of devoted laymen as leaders for Church and society in every walk of life. It fails in its duty if it returns to the home churches those who have been merely spoiled by their education and turned away from their native ground. Perhaps one of the chief distinctions of Christian education is that it gives no quarter to the 'intellectual' snob. It covers consecrated, grateful persons who know the daily debt in which their whole lives stand.

There can be, with some mutual.sympathy and under-standing, frequent exchanges back and forth, and some common awareness of their related task, the happiest kind of bond between the college and the Church. Each can do the other a great service. 'Religion needs the closest association with intellectual discipline and liberating in-sight, if its driving force is to make for humane life. It needs the repeated test of comparison with the ranges of known fact, to keep its drives relevant to the actual require-ments of human well-being in the actual world. It needs the critical temper of fine-edged minds constantly at work to keep its perspective clear, to make impossible its mistaking some partial, relative, created thing, human or inhuman, for the transcendent Reality that alone deserves adora-tion. This is why religion needs for its own good health a place in the enterprise of higher education, where the

intellectual life is especially cherished.'[14] Likewise, the
Church can help to maintain in its colleges a central
warmth and a devotion to Him whom they serve. He is
the beginning and the end of their adventure.

The whole future of the Church college depends, of
course, on whether it can survive at all. Many voices are
saying that the battle for all independent colleges, Church
or secular, is already lost — that they cannot hope to compete across the years with institutions receiving huge
grants from public funds. But as De Quincey once observed, 'To any man of regular habits it is disagreeable to
die.' Friends of private colleges will not, one believes, allow their death easily. There is divided opinion about
their acceptance of Federal aid — capital or operating
gifts, quite apart from any subsidy of worthy students in
the form of scholarships. Some Church colleges strongly
feel that they have a just claim on public funds — that
there is no legal barrier and that the public service they
render merits such support. It is not the purpose of this
book to debate this question, but the author must dis-
sociate himself from those who believe the future of our
Church colleges lies in any acceptance of Federal aid. He
warmly shares the view of the executive director of the
Association of American Colleges: 'It is a cause of grave
concern that [the Church] colleges are now inclined to
hold out their hands for Federal aid. It is axiomatic that
such assistance will involve a certain amount of Federal
control. Down that path inevitably lies a totalitarian type
of education and of government.'[15] As President Eisen-
hower likes to point out, a good government must follow
with real concern whatever money it spends. And that's
the trouble here. As education passes more and more to
the State, the private colleges, without disparaging the

great work done by public institutions vital to research and education, but out of a sheer principle of diversity, must believe themselves all the more needed. They are needed as active symbols and working leaven in a democracy that would keep its essential liberties. For a Church college, in particular, some of these liberties are indispensable. And whatever the trend of our national economy, and however relaxed about its own freedom the spirit of man may become in the second half of our century, we believe that the Church college in America will have its valiant friends.

One hopeful point, indeed, goes often unregarded. The colleges themselves can assist their own survival by the wise economy of tending to their own true knitting. They do not need atom smashers or the expensive equipment of universities. They can say no to the quixotic expansion of their curriculums, to those who wish to dignify every passing whim and caprice by making it a college subject. They can try to do a few things well rather than many things badly. They can try to live simply, though in good taste. They can spend what money they have on good men rather than on useless knickknacks. And in doing so, in addition to saving their lives, they may also save their souls. A great American scholar once said — and he was only half joking — 'The small colleges have so often given a good education because they were too poor to give a bad one.'

It is easy, however, to overstate the blessings of poverty, even when one has no Gargantuan dreams. If the Church colleges are not merely to survive but to become what they should become, the Church itself must catch some vision of them. President W. W. Peters reminded an audience not long ago of how strongly William Allen White, of Kansas, once expressed the whole matter:

Unless those who believe in a Christian civilization are willing to sacrifice of their good, hard-earned cash to educate Christian leaders, they will find in a few generations that their dream has vanished, that tyranny with its hard and fast ruthless rules of life will be substituted for the good life. It is not a question so much of churches and preachers alone as it is of these and colleges that will make leaders who will create a world in which churches can thrive, leaders in all walks of life, and in all callings and professions. If American churchmen fail to support the kinds of colleges that turn out Christian leaders, American life under another leadership soon will close the church.

Most Churches have never faced up to their educational task. In their membership they have wealth enough to put all their colleges on a first-class basis, and to give them a really creative life, to assure their being what Woodrow Wilson thought they were — 'the lighthouse of civilization.' He would not have thought it the business of churchmen to let their schools become somebody else's property or to be imperfect reminders of the noble intention that first gave them life when America was young and pioneering.

CHAPTER

5

THE LAST HALF OF THE CENTURY

MANY A MAN whose time and strength have never allowed him to get round to reading that 'great, still book' of the eighteenth century, Samuel Richardson's voluminous novel, *Clarissa Harlowe,* was comforted a few years ago by the observation of a compassionate literary critic. He suggested that here was a book to be read, not by individuals, but by generations. Each man in his time should do his stint, put in his bookmark, and go off to die content, leaving the next installment to his descendants. In some similar way, it is always comforting to know that no one generation, even our own, probably has to do all the unfinished business of mankind. There may be others after us. And, in their backward look at history, they may see our own hot and hectic time merely as one of the innumerable moments when a given decade or even a given century thought itself the climax of the human story.

Even so, our amiable descendants may well forgive anyone who in the year 1950 has thought himself at a mighty turning point in men's affairs. For, as we have earlier suggested, all men and women do now feel themselves part of some more than ordinary drama, whose background is life and death, good and evil, and whose stage is the whole world. What will the actors now say and do, what vision large or small will the chorus have, as the second half of our century moves forward?

It will be, or can be, some new act in the old story of Prometheus, who has always been for men a haunting symbol, whose effort and whose fate seem so much their own. In the *Prometheus Bound* of Aeschylus, the Titan steals the fire from heaven that men may better their condition and through new arts civilize themselves. The drama is not easy to interpret. But it sketches some mystery and puzzle of aspiring and not ignoble self-will pitted against eternal power and even eternal wisdom. Bound to his rock in the high Caucasus, the suffering Prometheus is a splendid, tragic figure. When, in later years, Shelley interpreted him in his *Prometheus Unbound,* he is the very protagonist of liberty against all manner of oppression.

Now, in our time, we rewrite the tragedy once more. Thus far it is a drama of humiliation. The Titan who won the gift of flame and the men for whom he won it have been made to hide in shelters and plan even greater shelters beneath the earth lest the enigmatic gift of fire destroy them. The whole proud industrial revolution goes underground. Men are become as moles; they have lived and may again live, not in the peaceful light of the sun nor on the surface of the earth over which, according to one account, they were given dominion. The chorus asks in bewilderment, 'Will you go on forever, like children, playing the game of bomb, bomb, who's got the bomb?' And the cynic snarls that what we need now is what *Punch* assured England a century ago was needed by people who worried over what to do in a railway accident when trains sped at thirty miles an hour — 'not presence of mind but complete absence of body.' *Prometheus Bound* was at least a noble title. But the name of our contemporary tragedy would be an ignoble one, perhaps *Prometheus Burrowing*. It is the awful symbol of our time. If we live through it and bring it to some resolution, even our descendants will know the depth we were in.

There is, thank heaven, more in men's hearts than a mere anxiety about survival. What gives a kind of distinction to our present crisis is the widening sense that the very saving of our skins depends on our securing a quality of life among men. This is the important mid-century news — this growing belief. It is bracing to the spirit when men think that what will save their lives will give also the quality that makes their lives worth saving. We have little faith left in gadgeteering. We have a growing mistrust of our devices. ' I remember,' says the old satirist, ' when our island was shaken with an earthquake some years ago, and an impudent mountebank sold us earthquake pills.' We have seen that some of our own panaceas have been earthquake pills of the first order. Miss Dorothy Thompson, for example, though she believes our civilization to be at its lowest point in a thousand years, has nevertheless a firm faith that we can yet give that civilization a new lease on life. ' Not might alone, nor money alone, nor technical power alone are power. Beyond all great revivals lies the intellectual, emotional, and spiritual power of an idea.' [1] The turning point of the history in which it is our privilege to share may well be this growing return of men to their minds and their souls. It is an unmistakable phenomenon of our day. It is much the best thing about us.

When the Western world, and more than the Western part, tries to express its highest idea, it wraps its hope in a single word — ' democracy.' By this it means far more than a form of government. It of course believes democracy to be the basis of government and of any international peace and order to which we may aspire. Primarily, the word 'democracy' expresses a conviction about man himself — that he has rights, duties, and meaning as a person. It would be false to claim that religion alone has nourished this conviction; but religion has had greatest influence in making it a common reality. Christianity, notably, has said important things about human nature. It saw in men, not equality of talent or ability, but an essential equality of human beings created by God in His image. That is now so deeply rooted that it will be a part of even the consciousness of an atheist. Aristotle held that some men were by nature slaves. To the apostle Paul, slavery was not illegal; but to him men were slaves only by accident of war — not through the nature of man, but by man's corruption. Cicero and his refined Roman contemporaries found a kind of equality in human beings because they could reason correctly and thus express a kind of universal reason operating through all things. But the democracy of seventeenth century England, and the democracy of Emerson and Whitman and Abraham Lincoln, had a more profound and more deeply human base. It was something more than political freedom — the freedom of those who felt themselves immortal persons of divine origin, valuing themselves even while they knew their dependence upon a power not themselves. Out of this they valued other persons also. It was not a democracy of logical heads, expressing some universal syllogism. It was a democracy of the sons of God, bound therefore in brotherhood, bearing His high mark upon their souls. John Marshall believed, of course, in abstract justice; but he attributed it to the Creator and held our Constitution to contain some divine ideas. A few years after him Justice Storey maintained that all high principles of society are eternal obligations arising from our common dependence upon God, and among these — as the prophet Micah saw in an earlier time — is our duty to do justly, to love mercy, and to walk humbly with our God. As Professor Hocking has brilliantly observed, democracy is a life that tries to combine a maximum of self-realization with a minimum of self-interest. This is the heart of Christianity. He has seen too that the practical working of a democratic state, as opposed to an anarchy, is change under law. The power of a vital religion is that it is, simultaneously, conservative and revolutionary. It sensitizes the conscience, creating respect for law; and it promotes change because it possesses an absolute, eternal standard for judging our imperfect relative procedures. This was the insight of our fathers.

When secularism abstracts the idea of democracy into a proposition or, on the other hand, makes it but one more experiment in man's natural groping toward some different condition from the one he has just been in, it abandons the view of personality out of which democracy has had its deepest sanction. This is why certain ardent defenders of civil liberties, anxious about the separation of Church and State, as many others are, should not worry too much, perhaps, about this principle's being violated by the singing of Christmas carols in classrooms. There are other splits possible in human nature that could do far more real harm to their liberal cause.

The 'theological myth,' we are told, is gone. Dr. Meiklejohn reminds us that 'in spite of all our protestations to the contrary, we have been busy for three hundred years' in making the State the successful rival of the Church.

Society has ' ousted religion and put government in its place. . . . In the transition from the medieval to the modern form of human living I doubt if any other change is as significant as the substitution of *political* teaching for *religious*. We have changed our procedure for determining what kind of beings human beings shall be.' [2] In higher education, which gives us the leaders of our democratic state, we are willing to regard religion as unessential or even as a nuisance. But we are still supposed to keep our democratic ideal going, out of some sense of kinship and worth among either animals, thinking machines, or creatures who, if they had all the vague, ideal qualities that secularism, in its nobler moments, attributes to them, would have so transcended their first cause that they would have cracked up all the logic reason ever knew. On this contemporary flimsy, democratic worth is optimistically supposed to rest.

Actually democracy is a homely, personal thing. It is the sum of what men think of themselves, of their common rights and duties. And nobody knows better than educators know that one of the important parts of any young person's education is a proper emphasis on the duties as well as the rights. In contemporary America we have heard far more about what people are owed than about what they owe. And secular education has contributed its part here — an easy equation of what is right with whatever succeeds, a stress on cleverness, on how to be smart.

Our colleges and universities founded in the name of truth had become the exponents of success. The measure of collegiate accomplishment was not in the moral rightness of the graduates but in the extent of their success, — the money they made, the positions they held, the influence they wielded, and the number recorded in *Who's Who*. . . . This then is the tragedy of our day that there is no party that would rather be true than to win an election, no nation that would rather be just than victorious, no candidate who would rather be right than president. . . . It is a startling fact that this doctrine of clever expediency has had its rise in the same period in which the college graduates have begun to dominate the scene.[3]

The freedom of a Christian is not the freedom just to be demanding or to exploit all the 'rights' and desires of his nature. It is a different kind of freedom, the freedom of a man who stands in relation, with his God and with his fellow men. He has practical communion and the life that flows from this communion. In the parable of the Ninety and Nine, the lost sheep is often regarded merely as a symbol of the value Christianity puts on the individual life. This, of course, is true. But, looked at more closely, the main fact about the lost sheep is that it was out of relationship with its shepherd. The communion of the fold was broken. And so with men. The gift of God, Christians feel, is a daily, eternal, common, magnificent bond of union. No life is lived separately or to its own desires. This is a democratic existence par excellence. The Christian claim to freedom 'carries with it the security against its own abuse; for it is freedom to serve God. Samuel Taylor Coleridge was profoundly right when he defined man's true freedom as " the power of the human being to maintain the obedience, which God through the conscience has commanded, against all the might of nature." ' [4]

This is the Christian realism about democracy — the realism of man as a person in relation with other persons. These last include both the living and the dead, and his sense of obligation to them is part of his sense of worth. No better advice has been given on this score than that President Arthur Coons of Occidental College gave his students, in the form of one of Goethe's wisest insights: 'What you have inherited from the fathers you must earn in order to possess.' These conceptions do justice to man's nature. They are deeply satisfying to the best we know when at our best. Democracy, and the wider democracy of a true international life, will have its last stand, not in a political abstraction, but 'in the realm of the people's faith.' [5] Religion is its 'inner citadel.'

One of the chief marks of democracy in America has been its zeal for providing education to all who can take advantage of it. Learning should not be the priority of any given class in society. President Conant has a remarkable paragraph in his latest book — one that should be widely known for its statement of what our temptation might have been:

A statesman of the sixteenth century, conversant with the history of the human race only to that time and suddenly dropped in the United States of 1900, might have asked some strange questions. He would have been particularly skeptical about the then current zeal for Americanization of the foreign-born. 'The recent immigrants,' he might have remarked, 'came here of their own free will. Certain nationalities, relative newcomers to this continent, have taken humble positions in a great industrial pattern. Some must be the hewers of wood, the drawers of water. Why not let these for-

eign immigrants and their descendants play this role?
Fate has solved for the United States the labor problem.' Our visitor might have continued, 'You did not
have to conquer another nation and make the outlanders
do your bidding — other nations have come to you for
this very purpose. Do not "Americanize" them; let
them keep their own cultures, their own languages; it
will be easier to place them in the social scale.' [6]

No such practical cynicism prevailed. As President Conant
says: 'A campaign of Americanization and of education
sprang forward on all sides. . . . Even today some may
wonder why when the tide of immigration was flowing
strong the older inhabitants strove to assimilate the newcomers on a basis of equality. Yet a failure to understand
the answer is a failure to understand the true nature of
our traditions.' [7]

This American dream of education open to all as far as
merit deserves has received its most striking statement, in
respect to higher learning, in the Report of the President's
Commission, completed in March, 1947, after some seven-
teen months of deliberation by twenty-seven members, assisted in their collection of data and opinion by many Government agencies and private organizations. It sets as a
goal for the American people an educational system which
will let no economic barrier prevent a qualified individual
anywhere in the country from attaining the kind of education he wants and can absorb. It sees our present normal
college and university enrollment of about a million and a
half going far beyond even our inflated postwar figure and
reaching, by 1960, some 4,600,000. A wide system of subsidy for the competent is, of course, involved.

We shall attempt here no examination of this Report. It

has had a mixed reception. Some have heralded with enthusiasm its democratic spirit and the sweep of its vision. Others have decried the inconsistencies in its internal logic, believed its estimate of those who can profit by higher education far too high, and felt its unconcern for private institutions and its exaltation of the state against the independent colleges — in spite of the Commission's occasional reminder that it wishes only well to these ' safeguards of our freedom ' that will be all the more needed if its Report is accepted and acted upon.

What is clear in the Report is its secular basis — no particular surprise in the kind of document it is. The Commission was not opening the Senate or laying a cornerstone and was therefore under no obligation to unite in prayer. It covets for Americans good behavior, ' based on ethical principles consistent with democratic ideals,' and sees the usefulness of ' a common cultural heritage toward a common citizenship.' [8] It passes on, apparently as a rumor, the fact that ' religion is held to be a major force in creating the system of human values on which democracy is predicated.' [9] It is concerned almost dangerously with the production of citizens who can realize certain social goals — dangerous, in spite of all the Report's talk about the ' free citizen,' his self-discipline and appreciation of a wide range of values, because the ethical standards the citizen will have, if he follows the implication of the Report, will be the same utilitarian and relative standards that have put mankind in the mess it is now in.[10] The Commission is composed of high-minded men who, obviously, want more than that. But not even in a minority report or in an appendix have they dared say more than that. Again, we should feel no particular surprise. We have become accustomed to writing nobly of American ideals without either the historical accuracy or the common candor of recognizing that these ideals grew largely out of a mind and conscience that believed in God and in some eternal standards. Almost our subtlest form of self-deception is our amiable habit of talking about our 'cultural heritage' with the main inheritance left out.

If we are, within another ten years, going to have four and a half million students — or even two thirds of that number — in our institutions of higher learning, our first task is to see that the learning is productive of some greater wisdom than we have been giving to the students we normally have. If this century is really going to belong to the common man, let us give the common man something of his common possessions — the faith that confers community, the faith that has made man really free from all the lower orders that would enslave him. If we give him only the unrestrained law of his own nature and the conceit of his own highly limited self, if we give him in the last half of our century the morally inept, the culturally and spiritually denatured life he has known in the first half — the vague talk of ideals that have no warrant in the total picture of the secular world to which he is bound — all our grand schemes of education will be no extension of democracy or the American dream. It will be just a stepping up of the American nightmare.

It would be much easier, and perhaps more comfortable, to keep conviction and standards and anything so decisive as religion out of our higher learning. Fact-collecting, open-mindedness as an end of life, to be forever learning and never coming to a knowledge of the truth, is less arduous than reflective commitment. Reflection is easy and commitment is easy; but the two together — that is an educational task demanding the highest powers. For education that seeks intelligent conviction about the meaning of life and its ends is no food for babes. But education that does not seek it is hardly anything we can decently refer to as ' the higher learning.' And we have now reached the place where education must pass beyond the intellectual virtues of mere questing after truth into the higher intellectual virtue of living, even while the quest continues, by the best truth we have already discovered. And the Christian faith, by its history and its present power on human life, has a right to be considered with the truth we already have.

The last half of our century is likely to be a fruitful one, not just out of its best inquiry, but out of its best convictions. ' The higher learning in America has developed a broad urbanity, an all-engulfing tolerance, which finds it easy to be hospitable to everything except conviction — and genuine conviction, which must not be confused with intolerance, is one of the crying needs of our age.' [11] This conviction will never grow out of our tools and techniques, though the human beings who achieve it can be helped toward it by the benevolent goods in modern science. Even the enlightened reason needs something beyond itself to fashion recalcitrant human passions and the human will, for the will seems to have a freedom deeper than any freedom of the mind. It has in it a possible anarchy, at least, beyond any the reason has ever known. The problem of either individual or social salvation seems to come at last to be one of values and of loyalty to these values:

It is not a problem of being open-minded, or objective, or dispassionate, or of mental discipline, or of learning to suspend the judgment. It is a problem of loving and hating the proper things, a problem of call-

ing only beautiful things beautiful, a problem of cher-
ishing values of universal validity rather than those of
limited worth. . . . In other words, it is a religious
problem.[12]

To say this is to give, of course, no clinching arguments
for Christianity. But it does suggest the paucity of an education that refuses even to examine what those arguments
are and what has happened to human life where they
prevailed.

At least the enemies of democracy know the value of
conviction and the effect of moral power. John Foster
Dulles, out of a rich experience in international affairs,
says he has noticed two impressive facts: first, ' the relatively small amount of moral authority available at any
given point of time and in connection with any particular
problem'; [13] and, secondly, the enormous influence even
a little moral authority can exercise — an influence out of
all proportion to the number of persons who reflect it. In
the United Nations, he has observed, every nation there is
' afraid of being caught on the wrong side of a moral issue' [14] and does everything it can to make whatever position it adopts seem morally correct. There is, Mr. Dulles
says, a lot of hypocrisy about all this and much deliberate
confusion. And meantime the Soviet Communist Party
beats us at what could so easily have been our game. Using moral slogans and catchwords, exalting its own faith
into a new kind of ' religion,' it tries to capture men's
minds and loyalties. This is the Trojan horse ' with which
it would penetrate into our society.' [15] The Russians an-
nounced these slogans at a time when Christian nations so
called seemed to have lost their own hold on great principles. The power of the Soviet Communist Party in the

world, Mr. Dulles believes, 'is due to the fact that while in a sense the Soviet state moved into a power vacuum in Europe and Asia, the Soviet Communist Party has moved into a moral vacuum in the world.' [16]

Our secular relativism has had no more searching indictment. If our democratic faith is to prevail, and to make its way among all men in a decent world order, it must again attach itself to a faith deeper than itself — to the highest sanction we have for human worth and to a transcendent community of those whose discipline and affections are born of some higher love than that of either self or country, where there is 'neither Jew nor Greek, neither bond nor free.' To seek that community and to fashion men and women for it is the task of education. That Christianity has long performed this very task is what learning can no longer ignore.

And what of the Christianity that would be recognized by learning? What must it become in the last half of our century? Certainly it must transcend the bonds of narrow sectarianism and make its appeal to men in a form that outrages neither their common sense nor their own charity. An atomized religion can do little to stop the further atomization of the world. 'In our time, Christianity has become, for the first time, a world reality; and, in so doing, has become the first truly world movement this planet has known.' [17] The Roman Catholic Church has always had its universal sense. But now 'the major Protestant Churches have begun to see their tasks as one task; and have begun so to face it, and to plan and work together, as though the Christian churches were One Church, truly a Body of Christ.' [18] All this has meaning for culture as well as for religion.

Christianity will make its way in men's imaginations if

it reveals itself as more than a set of rules. Without losing its ethical character or its moral power, it can show that its secret is more than the secret of renunciation. It suffers, among young people especially, from the suggestion it too often gives of spiritual pride, tight-lipped respectability, or a tidy goodness that lacks humor, sympathy, and understanding, and any human sense of how life can knock and batter at the bodies and souls of men. It is, as has been said, morality lighted up with something else — with a life-bestowing bond of man to a power beyond himself. It is the morality of a heart and will regenerated in a new relationship. For faith, in Newman's superb insight, is 'a habit of the soul,' a practical keeping alive of such a sustained and full communion with God that every instinct of the spirit, in all daily tasks and experience, is in perpetual reference to Him. This becomes a working principle of living in which 'life, law, joy, impulse are one thing.' One of the finest religious insights of recent years has, in this connection, been that of a university teacher:

I think all Christians would agree with me if I said that though Christianity seems at first to be all about morality, all about duties and rules and guilt and virtue, yet it leads you on, out of all that, into something beyond. One has a glimpse of a country where they don't talk of those things, except perhaps as a joke. Every one there is filled full with what we should call goodness as a mirror is filled with light. But they don't call it goodness. They don't call it anything. They are not thinking of it. They are too busy looking at the source from which it comes. But this is near the stage where the road passes over the rim of our world. No one's eyes can see very far beyond that: though lots of people's eyes can see further than mine.[19]

No heavenly contemplation or bond of divine relation ship will relieve the Christian, however, of his task in this world. It was one of our greatest mystics who reminded us that ' the Church must face the real issues of life and make a practical difference in the lives of actual men and women and children, or it is doomed to become a disappearing affair.' [20] Its work is in the social order also. If it believes that order is a sacred thing and not secular, it must do more for it than a secularist would do. And, in its sense of its own strength, it must not pridefully alienate itself from secular wisdom and secular techniques. These too to the Christian become sacred and his only response is to be grateful for what any man has done for other men.

Nor need the Christian renounce that life of reason so dear to humanism. Any sense he has of sin and human pride, or of reason's own corruption, need not let him believe that the light of his mind is all darkness. The Christian's mistrust of rationalism as the sole instrument of truth should not link him with the forces of irrationality. To become incapable of or superior to all logical effort, to despise all critical examination, to cut himself off from the human assault on ignorance and befuddlement is to renounce the mind God gave him. Nothing is more realistic than the Christian's sense of sin and his utter need of divine grace and forgiveness. His failure is an involved failure — not just of reason, but of passion and will. Redemption is his solid and only ultimate answer to the riddle of evil. But a romanticizing of his own depravity as a ticket of leave from hard intellectual work, from his own partnership with God's own preference for light over darkness, is to renounce his own creatureship. A 'fallen' mind is not an extinct or hopeless one. It can still struggle toward the light. The problem of what is still good in man is as important as the problem of what is evil. He is still the shining enigma, whom God reaches down to help. Something of this was what Milton saw in his picture of the angel Michael's sending Adam out of Paradise. Michael had a comforting word — that by his reason, among other of his efforts, man would someday build within himself an Eden happier far than any he had known; that the last sight beheld by mortal eyes would not necessarily be a sword blazing as the sign of man's humiliation above a paradise that he had lost. This can still be a common faith for both Christianity and liberal education.

But the final claim of Christianity on men and on universities is not a thought. It is the reality of Jesus Christ — His revelation of the love of God and of immortal life. If Christianity be merely another phase of the 'good life,' and Jesus but another good man, the university has only relative need to take account of it. University archives are full of theories about the good life and of the histories of good men. Philosophy and noble biography are not new.

If Christianity, on the other hand, offers Jesus as what He said He was, that is something else again. That is something unique in life and in liberal education. More than churchmen are beginning to see that a God revealed in a person is no constricted deity, no inferior revelation. It is a revelation more profound and right than any other could be. A child born in a manger can be more impressive than the stars in their courses, and the cross is a symbol not inferior to a formula in mathematics. Eternity itself is not grander as a conception than the stunning event in time that blazed forth the love that moves the sun and the other stars, the love that brought man and God together. God's giving man the supreme image of Himself as a man was the most universal expression possible of any universal truth. In the vast storehouse of being there may be some other revelation. But, earthbound, man already has one that he can understand. It is one in which the meaning of his own life is most likely to be found.

This is the Christian claim on the world's attention. And it is not just the record of the incarnation alone, but its effect on all subsequent history. For Christianity has struck the life of man, not just as some charming story out of time, but as a revolution out of eternity. Its haunting symbols and pastoral images — the manger with its holy light, the shepherds watching their flocks by night, the dark figures bearing gifts to the shining lady and the luminous child — these are not just beautiful and tender images cherished among our memories. They have about them an awful virility, 'terrible as an army with banners,' for all who comprehend them. Out of that early century have gone a passion and a force that have changed human life and remade the human mind. The Christian revelation has its record in all culture — in art and music and architecture; it has healed men everywhere and made the rough places plain; it has altered the face of nations. It has resisted evil and oppression and conquered hate with love. It has its martyrs and disciples, plain men with superb scorn for death; and it has given to philosophers new argument for life. It has persisted beyond all effort to pervert it and to make its abiding secret other than what it is.

That secret is immortal love transforming the lives of men. This is the law of all being, as the Christian sees it — the supreme hope he has for the last half of our century.

This was the *new thing*, and no one was more aware of its newness than Jesus was. One day, according to the account in the fourth chapter of the Gospel of Luke:

> He came to Nazareth, where he had been brought up: and, as his custom was, he went into the synagogue on the sabbath day, and stood up for to read. And there was delivered unto him the book of the prophet Esaias. And when he had opened the book, he found the place where it was written,
>
>> The Spirit of the Lord is upon me,
>> Because he hath anointed me
>> To preach the gospel to the poor;
>> He hath sent me to heal the broken-hearted,
>> To preach deliverance to the captives,
>> And recovering of sight to the blind,
>> To set at liberty them that are bruised,
>> To preach the acceptable year of the Lord.
>
> And he closed the book, and he gave it again to the minister, and sat down.

What Jesus had been reading was the beginning of the sixty-first chapter of Isaiah. It goes about as He read it. Maybe it is only a fancy to think that He shut the book and did not read on not merely because He had finished the statement of His own appointment. He broke off, one observes, in the middle of a sentence. For Isaiah reads:

> 'To proclaim the acceptable year of the Lord,
> And the day of vengeance of our God.'

Perhaps on that occasion, back home among His own people, Jesus felt more than usual how the old law had been transcended, how justice even had been tempered by the power of the new secret He carried in His heart. He had something new to tell men — that God's love for them and their love for God and their neighbor is the meaning and fulfillment of their lives. Out of this they can even yet repair the waste cities and the desolations of many generations.

This, at any rate, is what Christianity has to say to the last half of our century. It may be hard for the higher learning to think of anything more intelligent.

REFERENCES

REFERENCES

CHAPTER 1

1. See G. M. Young, *Early Victorian England 1830–1865*, vol. i, pp. 212 ff. Oxford University Press, 1934.
2. See Louis Arnaud Reid, '*Vocational*' and '*Humane*' *Education in the University*, University Pamphlets No. 11, p. 26. S. C. M. Press, Ltd., 1946.
3. Dorothy Sayers, *Creed or Chaos?*, p. 70. Harcourt, Brace and Company, 1949.
4. Arnold J. Toynbee, *A Study of History*, vol. vi, p. 320. Oxford University Press, 1939.
5. Howard Mumford Jones, *Education and World Tragedy*, pp. 3, 5, 7, 9. Harvard University Press, 1946.
6. Emmanuel Mounier, 'Reflections on an Apocalyptic Age,' in *The Nineteenth Century*, 144 (September, 1948), p. 152.
7. William Butler Yeats, 'The Resurrection,' in *Wheels and Butterflies*, p. 115. The Macmillan Company, 1935.
8. Editorial, *The Cleveland News*, June 9, 1949.
9. Dorothy Thompson, *The Developments of Our Times*, The Merrill Lectures, 1948, p. 15. John B. Stetson University, The University Press, 1948.
10. Dixon Wecter, *Quality and the Independent College*, Founder's Day Address, Pomona College Bulletin, November, 1948, vol. xlvi, no. 3, p. 9.
11. Quoted by Alexander Dallin, in 'The Fateful Pact: Prelude to World War II,' *The New York Times Magazine*, August 21, 1949, p. 11.
12. Robert Worth Frank, 'Where Secularism Fails,' in *McCormick Speaking*, 1, no. 5 (March, 1948), p. 4.
13. *Ibid.*, p. 6.
14. Lewis Mumford, *The Condition of Man*, p. 380. Harcourt, Brace and Company, 1944.

15. Carl L. Becker, *The Heavenly City of the Eighteenth-Century Philosophers*, pp. 30–31. Yale University Press, 1932.
16. Bronislaw Malinowski's lecture, 'The Foundation of Faith and Morals,' quoted by Luther Weigle, in 'The American Tradition and the Relation between Religion and Education,' *American Council on Education Studies*, vol. ix, series 1, no. 2, February, 1945, p. 29.
17. B. M. G. Reardon, 'On a Christian Theory of Education,' in *The Fortnightly*, 165 (n.s. 159; January, 1946), p. 64.
18. William Temple, *The Hope of a New World*, p. 64. The Macmillan Company, 1942.
19. William Van Buskirk, 'New Emphases and a New Epoch,' typed copy of lecture, p. 2.
20. T. S. Eliot, chorus from *The Rock*, p. 30. Harcourt, Brace and Company, 1934.
21. I. L. Kandel, quoted by J. Paul Williams, in *The New Education and Religion*, p. 1. Association Press, 1945.
22. Robert M. Hutchins, *Education for Freedom*, p. 47. Louisiana State University Press, 1944.
23. Quoted by E. La Mothe Stowell, 'Pseudo-Religions and Reconversion,' in *The Hibbert Journal*, 46, no. 1 (October, 1947), p. 29.
24. See Hugh S. Taylor, 'Science, Education, and Human Values,' *Association of American Colleges Bulletin*, 35, no. 1 (March, 1949), pp. 30–31.
25. Tennessee College Association; proceedings of 1943 meeting, p. 35.
26. Norman Cousins, *Trustees of the Human Race*, address at inauguration of Homer Price Rainey as president of Stephens College, November 8, 1948, p. 3.
27. Quoted by Roland Renne in inaugural address as president of Montana State College, April 10, 1945.
28. H. S. Canby, in *The Saturday Review of Literature*, April 24, 1948, p. 20.

CHAPTER 2

1. From *New England's First Fruits*, reprinted in Samuel Eliot Morison, *The Founding of Harvard College*, p. 432. Harvard University Press, 1935.
2. See Morison, *op. cit.*, p. 183.
3. *Ibid.*, pp. 248, 249.
4. *Ibid.*, p. 8.

5. *Ibid.*, pp. 247–248, 250.
6. *Ibid.*, p. 251.
7. See Charles F. Thwing, *A History of Higher Education in America*, pp. 47–48, Appleton, 1906.
8. Morison, *op. cit.*, pp. 250–260.
9. For the whole story of religion on the campus until 1900, see *Two Centuries of Religious Activity at Yale*, edited by James B. Reynolds, Samuel H. Fisher, and Henry B. Wright. G. P. Putnam's Sons, 1901.
10. Lyman Beecher, cited by Reynolds *et al.*, *Two Centuries of Religious Activity at Yale*, p. 53.
11. See *Samuel Johnson, President of King's College, His Career and Writings*, edited by Herbert and Carol Schneider, vol. iv, p. 223. Columbia University Press, 1929.
12. See Thwing, *op. cit.*, pp. 112 ff.
13. Albea Godbold, *The Church College of the Old South*, pp. 178–179. Duke University Press, 1944.
14. *Ibid.*, p. 180.
15. *Ibid.*, pp. 180–181, 178.
16. Thwing, *op. cit.*, p. 285.
17. Godbold, *op. cit.*, p. 53.
18. *Ibid.*, p. 67, quoting *Christian Index*, February 18, 1836.
19. Donald G. Tewksbury, *The Founding of American Colleges and Universities Before the Civil War*, p. 90. Bureau of Publications, Teachers College, Columbia University, 1932.
20. Merle Curti, *The Social Ideas of American Educators*, quoted by J. Paul Williams, *op. cit.*, pp. 50–51.
21. Thwing, *op. cit.*, p. 229.
22. Leon Burr Richardson, *History of Dartmouth College*, vol. i, pp. 275–276. Dartmouth College Publications, 1932.
23. Henry P. Van Dusen, 'Education and Christian Faith,' *Christian Education*, 31, no. 2 (June, 1948), p. 85.
24. Robert M. Hutchins, *op. cit.*, p. 25.
25. Howard Mumford Jones, 'Religious Education in the State Universities,' in *Religion and Education*, edited by Willard L. Sperry, p. 70. Harvard University Press, 1945.
26. Van Dusen, *op. cit.*, p. 84.
27. Jacques Barzun, 'Harvard Takes Stock,' in *The Atlantic Monthly*, 176 (October, 1945), p. 52.
28. *Ibid.*
29. *General Education in a Free Society*, Report of the Harvard Committee, p. 43. Harvard University Press, 1945.
30. *Ibid.*, p. 38.

31. *Ibid.*, p. 70.
32. *Ibid.*, p. 65.
33. *Ibid.*, p. 48.
34. *Ibid.*, p. 76.
35. *Ibid.*, p. 174.
36. *Ibid.*, p. 39.
37. *Ibid.*, p. 46.
38. *Ibid.*, p. 76.
39. E. Fay Campbell in address.
40. F. G. Peabody, 'Voluntary Chapel,' in *The Development of Harvard University Since the Inauguration of President Eliot, 1869–1929,* edited by S. E. Morison, p. lvii. Harvard University Press, 1930.
41. Merrimon Cuninggim, *The College Seeks Religion,* p. 65. Yale University Press, 1947.
42. *Ibid.*
43. Charles F. Wishart, in *On Going to College,* p. 230. Oxford University Press, 1938.
44. *General Education in a Free Society,* p. 40.
45. *Ibid.*, p. 45.
46. *Ibid.*, p. 211.
47. *Ibid.*, p. 69.
48. *Ibid.*, p. 71.
49. *Ibid.*, p. 72.
50. *Ibid.*
51. *Ibid.*, pp. 77, 78.
52. *Ibid.*, p. viii.
53. *Ibid.*, p. 151.
54. Charles W. Gilkey, 'The Place of Religion in Higher Education,' in *Religion and the Modern World,* University of Pennsylvania Bicentennial Conference, p. 74. University of Pennsylvania Press, 1941.
55. Charles Seymour, inaugural address; see *School and Society,* 46, no. 1190 (October 16, 1937), p. 485.
56. Harold W. Dodds, *A Report by the President to the Board of Trustees on Princeton's Religious Program.*
57. Professor Clarence Shedd has also given a valuable study in his books, *Two Centuries of Christian Student Movements* and *The Church Follows Its Students.*
58. Cuninggim, *op. cit.*, p. 1.
59. *Ibid.*, p. 23.
60. *Ibid.*, p. 46.
61. *Ibid.*, p. 250.

62. See the report by President John W. Nason, of Swarthmore College, in pamphlet published by the Edward J. Hazen Foundation, reprinting from *The Educational Record*, October, 1946; and see also Albert C. Outler, *Colleges, Faculties and Religion*, Hazen Pamphlet, January, 1949.
63. Nason, in Hazen Pamphlet, p. 11.
64. Outler, *op. cit.*, pp. 13–14.
65. Nason, *op. cit.*, p. 6.
66. Outler, *op. cit.*, p. 15.
67. Cuninggim, *op. cit.*, p. 150.

CHAPTER 3

1. L. P. Eisenhart, *The Educational Process*, p. 14. Princeton University Press, 1945.
2. Harold W. Dodds, *Out of This Nettle, Danger . . .* , p. 48. Princeton University Press, 1943.
3. *Ibid.*, p. 53.
4. See report by Louis Gale, *Cleveland Plain Dealer*, August 21, 1949.
5. Matthew Arnold, 'The Function of Criticism at the Present Time,' in *Essays in Criticism*, p. 12. The Macmillan Company, 1924.
6. *Ibid.*, p. 15.
7. Spencer Leeson, *Christian Education*, p. 111. Longmans, Green & Co., Inc., 1947.
8. George F. Thomas, 'The Responsibility of the University for Religious Instruction' (typescript).
9. H. A. Hodges, *Objectivity and Impartiality*, University Pamphlets No. 2, p. 27. S. C. M. Press, Ltd., 1946. The entire pamphlet is worth reading.
10. Sidney Hook, in *The American Scholar* 15, no. 1 (Winter, 1945–1946), p. 113.
11. Edwin H. Rian, *Christianity and American Education*, p. 96. The Naylor Company, 1949. See pp. 98–107 for his examination of school and college textbooks reflecting a naturalistic view of life.
12. George A. Buttrick, *Christ and Man's Dilemma*, p. 138. Abingdon-Cokesbury Press, 1946.
13. Van Buskirk, *op. cit.*
14. Lionel Trilling, in *New York Times Book Review*, September 4, 1949, p. 5.

15. John Henry Newman, *On the Scope and Nature of University Education*, Everyman Edition, p. 89. J. M. Dent, 1915.
16. Stuart P. Sherman, 'Samuel Butler: Diogenes of the Victorians,' *Points of View*, p. 271. Charles Scribner's Sons, 1924.
17. T. M. Greene *et al.*, *Liberal Education Re-examined*, p. 67. Harper & Brothers, 1943.
18. Quoted by Arnold S. Nash, *The University and the Modern World*, p. 259. The Macmillan Company, 1944.
19. Matthew Arnold, 'Pagan and Mediaeval Religious Sentiment,' *op. cit.*, p. 197.
20. Percival R. Cole, *A History of Educational Thought*, p. 100. Oxford University Press, 1931.
21. Reinhold Niebuhr, 'Religion and Modern Knowledge,' in *Man's Destiny in Eternity*, The Garvin Lectures, p. 127. The Beacon Press, Inc., 1949.
22. Henry Churchill King, *Personal and Ideal Elements in Education*, p. 78. The Macmillan Company, 1904.
23. A comprehensive and well-detailed account of various programs is given in Merrimon Cuninggim's *The College Seeks Religion*.
24. John Baillie, *The Mind of the Modern University*, University Pamphlets No. 1, p. 35. S. C. M. Press, Ltd., 1946.
25. Daniel T. Jenkins, *The Place of a Faculty of Theology in the University of To-day*, University Pamphlets No. 8, pp. 16–17. S. C. M. Press, Ltd., 1946.
26. Nason, *op. cit.*, p. 8.
27. Robert M. Hutchins, typescript of address (to be published shortly by Kenyon College).
28. Greene *et al.*, *op. cit.*, pp. 67–68.
29. Bernard Iddings Bell, 'Studying Religion in the Universities,' in *The Christian Century*, 65, no. 38 (September 22, 1948), pp. 973, 974.

CHAPTER 4

1. See Spencer Leeson, *op. cit.*, p. 108.
2. Samuel Eliot Morison and Henry Steele Commager, *The Growth of the American Republic*, vol. i, pp. 409–410. Oxford University Press, 1937.
3. Frank H. Caldwell, 'Christian Education, the Church, and I,' address at Inauguration of President Walter Groves, of Centre College, pp. 86, 87.
4. John Henry Newman, *op. cit.*, pp. 27, 61.

5. W. Norman Pittenger, 'Religion and the College,' in *The Christian Century*, 61, no. 7 (February 16, 1944), p, 202.
6. Charles W. Gilkey, ' Religion for the Modern Mind,' a summary of a Conference of Church Workers, in *Religion in Higher Education*, edited by M. C. Towner, p. 88. University of Chicago Press, 1931.
7. H. H. Horne, *The Philosophy of Christian Education*, p. 169. Fleming H. Revell Company, 1937.
8. Thornton Wilder, *The Woman of Andros*, p. 55. Boni & Liveright, 1930.
9. Albert C. Outler, *A Christian Context for Counseling*, Hazen Pamphlet, p. 3.
10. *Ibid.*
11. Matthew Arnold, 'Pagan and Mediaeval Religious Sentiment,' *op. cit.*, p. 220.
12. Sir Arthur Quiller-Couch, *On the Art of Reading*, p. 37. G. P. Putnam's Sons, 1920.
13. Arthur G. Coons, *Why Are We Here?*, convocation address at Occidental College, p. 13.
14. Robert L. Calhoun, 'The Place of Religion in Higher Education,' in *Religion and the Modern World*, University of Pennsylvania Bicentennial Conference, p. 70. University of Pennsylvania Press, 1941.
15. Guy E. Snavely, 'The Church-Related College in the Atomic Age,' address delivered at inauguration of President Franc L. McCluer, Lindenwood College, October 23, 1947, p. 7.

CHAPTER 5

1. Dorothy Thompson, *op. cit.*, p. 27.
2. Alexander Meiklejohn, 'From Church to State,' in *Religion and Education*, edited by Willard L. Sperry, pp. 3, 4. Harvard University Press, 1945.
3. Ralph Cooper Hutchison, 'Educational Obligation of the Church,' in *The Presbyterian Tribune*, 61, no. 10 (July, 1946), pp. 16–17.
4. William Temple, *op. cit.*, p. 25.
5. Charles Clayton Morrison, quoted by J. Paul Williams, *op. cit.*, p. 161.
6. James Bryant Conant, *Education in a Divided World*, p. 12. Harvard University Press, 1948.
7. *Ibid.*, pp. 13, 14.
8. *Higher Education for American Democracy*, A Report of the

President's Commission on Higher Education, vol. i, pp. 50, 49. Washington, December, 1947.

9. *Ibid.*, i, p. 50.
10. For analysis, see Gould Wickey, 'The President Studies Higher Education,' in *Christian Education*, 31, no. 2 (June, 1948).
11. Robert M. Hutchins, 'The Relation of Religion to Public Education,' by the Committee on Religion and Education of the American Council on Education, series i, no. 26, April, 1947, p. 41.
12. Hugh Stevenson Tigner, 'The Pretensions of Science,' in *The Christian Century*, 55, no. 37 (September 14, 1938), p. 1097.
13. John Foster Dulles, 'Moral Force in World Affairs,' in *Presbyterian Life*, April 10, 1948, p. 13.
14. *Ibid.*, p. 30.
15. *Ibid.*, p. 29.
16. *Ibid.*, p. 28.
17. Henry P. Van Dusen, 'Our Christian World Task,' *Christian Education*, 32, no. 1 (March, 1949), p. 1.
18. *Ibid.*
19. C. S. Lewis, *Christian Behaviour*, p. 70. The Macmillan Company, 1944.
20. Rufus Jones, 'The Church as an Organ of Social Ideas,' in *Religion and the Modern World*, University of Pennsylvania Bicentennial Conference, p. 117. University of Pennsylvania Press, 1941.